JOURNEY THROUGH JEWISH HISTORY

SEYMOUR ROSSEL

BEHRMAN HOUSE, INC.
Publishers & Booksellers / New Jersey

THE AGE OF FAITH AND THE AGE OF FREEDOM

JOURNEY THROUGH JEWISH HISTORY

SEYMOUR ROSSEL

ILLUSTRATED BY
KATHERINE KAHN

ACKNOWLEDGMENTS

The author wishes to express his gratitude to the following people: Dr. David Ruderman who read the materials relating to the medieval period; Dr. Steve Zipperstein who read the materials relating to the modern period. Their scholarship was in all cases edifying; their friendship sustaining. Mr. Neal Kozodoy read the entire manuscript, making many fine suggestions and helping to solidify the whole. And my wife, Karen Trager Rossel, styled the final manuscript with her incomparable patience and insight. I am especially grateful to Mr. Jacob Behrman for the great confidence he placed in me, allowing me the opportunity to prepare these two volumes. S.R.

PROJECT EDITOR RALPH DAVIS

COVER AND CONSULTATION BY ROBERT O'DELL
MAPS BY JOSEPH ASCHERL
PHOTO CREDITS

American Jewish Historical Society 90, 91 / The Bettman Archive 43, 95 / Biblioteca Apostalica, Vatican City / Bibliotheque Nationale 22 upper left, 25 / British Library 51 left / Consulate General of Israel 138, 140, 141, 143 / Darmsteadter, Frank J. 17, 30, 59, 65, 141, 105 / Davis, Ralph 51 right, 95 right / Editorial Photocolor Archives 23, 150 center / Hadassah 132 / Halliday, Sonia 49 / Harris, David contents, 7, Unit Heads: Frontspiece of the Schocken Bible of the 13th century, from South Germany, Schocken Institute, Jerlusalem 9, 74, 135, 136, 137, 145, 146 / Herzog August Bibliothek, West Germany 27 / Hopf, John T., Newport 85 / Jewish Museum 98, 99 / Jewish Reconstructionist Foundation 153 / UAHC 11, 129 / Metropolitan Museum of Art 65 / Religious News Service 150 upper left, lower / Reproducaanes, MAS, Barcelona 15 / Rosegarten Museum 30, 31 / Rossel, Seymour 152 / Slavin, Emma 54 / Sonnenfeld, Leni 8, 71, 75, 114, 119 lower, 124, 130, 131B, 134, 138, 150 / Theological Seminary of America 22 lower / Torah Umeresorah 152 / YIVO 97, 119, 125 / YOAV-Phototake 8 lower center, 245 / Zionist Archives 80, 113, 115, 118, 121, 127 / Zlotowitz, Bernard 142 /

PUBLISHED BY BEHRMAN HOUSE, INC.
Springfield, New Jersey 07081
www.behrmanhouse.com

MANUFACTURED IN THE UNITED STATES OF AMERICA

DEDICATION

For Amy and Deborah,
whose journey
is just beginning —

Library of Congress Cataloging in Publication Data
(Revised for book 2)
Rossel, Seymour.
Journey through Jewish history.
Contents: Bk. 1. From covenant to sages—Bk. 2. The Age of Faith and the Age of Freedom.
1. Jews—History—Juvenile literature. [1. Jews—History] I. Title.
DS118.R592   1981   909'.04924   81-3902
ISBN 0-87441-335-4 (v. 1)
ISBN 0-87441-367-2 (v. 2)

CONTENTS

HOW IT ALL BEGAN

As a Jew today, you belong to a community of people who are concerned about one another and who share important beliefs, ideas, and values. If you live in a country that is part of the free world—such as England, Canada, Australia, Israel, the United States—you are concerned about Jews who live in places like Russia, Syria, and Ethiopia, where there is little or no freedom. Jews everywhere care deeply about

what happens to the Jewish state, the State of Israel. Indeed, if we could stretch threads from our local synagogue or community center to all the Jewish communities and people about whom we care and whom we love, the threads would surround the planet Earth like a vast web.

But our Jewish way of life—what we believe, what we treasure, what we remember—was not shaped all at once. It grew out of a great journey through time and place.

A Bukharian Jew

A Yemenite Jew

A Turkish Jew

To show all our concerns, we would have to weave our threads back into the past, stitching a web through thousands of years and hundreds of Jewish communities, many of which long ago disappeared. All of these communities helped to shape us in one way or another, helped to make us the kind of people we are today. And we would have to spin a web into the future, to communities and places we can only imagine. For Jewish cares and concerns are very much involved with what the future will be. We want it to be good—for Jews, and for all human beings—just as Jews throughout the ages have dreamed that we would live in freedom and that the Jews would return to the Land of Israel to rebuild it.

Perhaps you can imagine it in another way: We are like mountain climbers and our history is the story of our climb thus far. Those of us living today are tied together in order that we may help one another along. We have climbed high up the mountain. Still, we cannot see the top. We hope that once we reach it many things will be explained by the view that greets our eyes. And that is why we climb—because it is a holy mountain, and the top of it is surely a sacred place.

This is not a new idea. It comes from the words of the prophets Isaiah and Micah. They said (Isa. 2:2–3; Mic. 4:1–2)

> *In the days to come,*
> *The Mount of the Lord's House*
> *Shall stand firm above the mountains . . .*
> *And the many peoples shall go and say:*
> *"Come,*
> *Let us go up to the Mount of the Lord. . ."*

The many faces of our people.

An Ethiopian Jew

A Jew from Eastern Europe

The Bible   Our first history book was the Bible. It tells us how we began. A man named Abraham and a woman named Sarah made a covenant with the One God who promised to make them a great nation and to give them the Land of Israel as a possession forever. In return, they promised to follow God's way: to be just and kind and faithful. Even today we recite this covenant; so any history of our people that will make sense for us today must begin with the story of Abraham and Sarah.

And it must continue with the story of Moses, the Egyptian prince who led the Israelites into the desert, who brought them to Mount Sinai where they made a covenant between God and the people Israel for all times. The Bible tells how Moses wrote the five books of the Torah, led the people to the borders of the Holy Land, and was the beloved prophet of the Lord. We still live by the covenant and the teachings of Moses; so any true history of our people must include this story.

Many scholars believe that the mountain called Sinai in the Bible is far to the north, but through the ages pilgrims have come to the jagged mountaintop called Sinai seen above over the desert hills.

The Bible and History

Archaeologists, those who study the past through what people left behind, have found evidence for most of what the Bible tells us. The Promised Land was slowly conquered by the Jews. The stories of the Judges—Gideon, Samson, Deborah, Samuel, and others—are true to the life of their times. We know there were great battles between the peoples called the Philistines and the Jews, battles led by Israel's first kings, Saul and David. And archaeologists have uncovered the ruins of many great cities and monuments such as those King Solomon built.

We can trace the history of the divided kingdoms of Israel in the north and Judah to the south; and we know that the ten tribes of the north were taken captive by the Assyrians in 722 B.C.E., disappearing forever. The Temple in Jerusalem was destroyed in 586 B.C.E. by the armies of Nebuchadnezzar; and many of the Jews of Judah were taken to Babylonia where they sat and wept, remembering Zion their homeland.

But Babylonia, too, was conquered by a mighty empire, the Persians. And Cyrus the Great, king of Persia, allowed the Jews to return to Jerusalem to rebuild their nation and their Temple. Though many stayed in Babylonia, some returned to Israel and established the second commonwealth, a new Jewish state.

The Jews and the Synagogue

More conquerers came, the Greeks and the Romans. Bitter wars were fought when they tried to put an end to the Jewish religion. At last, mighty Rome destroyed the Second Temple in the year 70 C.E. The Romans believed they had put an end

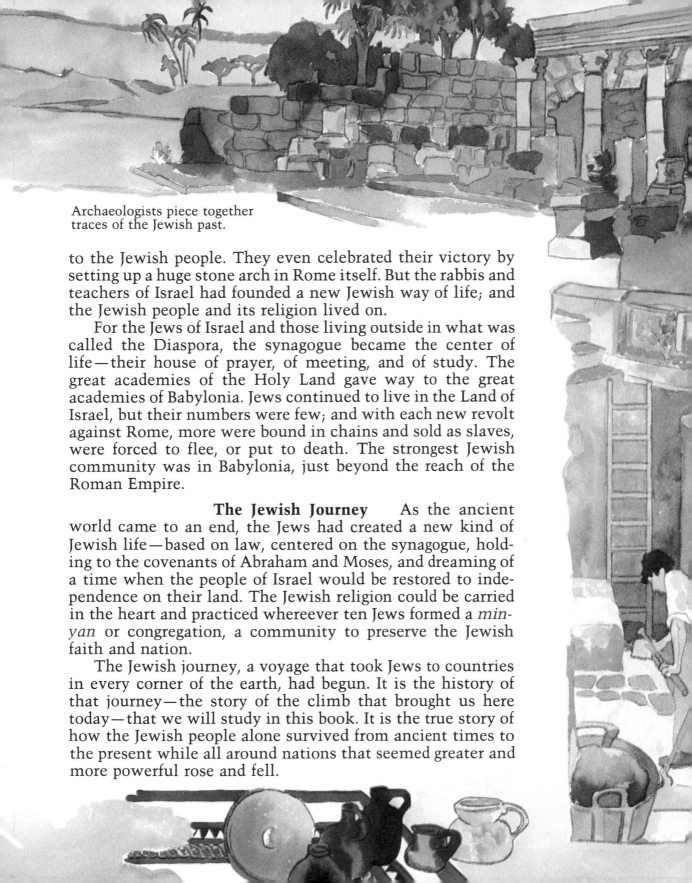

Archaeologists piece together traces of the Jewish past.

to the Jewish people. They even celebrated their victory by setting up a huge stone arch in Rome itself. But the rabbis and teachers of Israel had founded a new Jewish way of life; and the Jewish people and its religion lived on.

For the Jews of Israel and those living outside in what was called the Diaspora, the synagogue became the center of life—their house of prayer, of meeting, and of study. The great academies of the Holy Land gave way to the great academies of Babylonia. Jews continued to live in the Land of Israel, but their numbers were few; and with each new revolt against Rome, more were bound in chains and sold as slaves, were forced to flee, or put to death. The strongest Jewish community was in Babylonia, just beyond the reach of the Roman Empire.

The Jewish Journey As the ancient world came to an end, the Jews had created a new kind of Jewish life—based on law, centered on the synagogue, holding to the covenants of Abraham and Moses, and dreaming of a time when the people of Israel would be restored to independence on their land. The Jewish religion could be carried in the heart and practiced whereever ten Jews formed a *minyan* or congregation, a community to preserve the Jewish faith and nation.

The Jewish journey, a voyage that took Jews to countries in every corner of the earth, had begun. It is the history of that journey—the story of the climb that brought us here today—that we will study in this book. It is the true story of how the Jewish people alone survived from ancient times to the present while all around nations that seemed greater and more powerful rose and fell.

THE JEWS AND TORAH

The prophets taught that God loved kindness and justice more than the animal sacrifices of the Temple. The Pharisees—sages and rabbis—taught the people to read and write, taught them Torah, and taught them the traditions that had been handed from generation to generation by word of mouth. The people studied the law of the two torahs—the written Torah of Moses, and the spoken or Oral Torah taught by the Pharisees.

In time, the Oral Torah was written down, too. The sages—Hillel, Akiba, Meir, and Rabbi Judah the Prince—made the first collections, which became the Mishnah. The rabbis in the Holy Land collected more Oral Torah and gave us the Jerusalem (or Palestinian) Talmud. And the Babylonian rabbis collected a work that became the guide for Jewish life from that time to this, the Babylonian Talmud.

While other nations continued to believe that conquering territory was the most important thing, the Jews taught that following God's law and keeping the covenant was more important. They measured greatness not by might in war, but by peace; not in warriors but in students. And they hoped that other nations would see the wisdom of their ways, would set aside the weapons of war, and take up the study of peace instead.

The Babylonian sages discussed great and small matters with equal devotion. Every detail of the Jewish way of life is important.

1 LIFE IN THE MIDDLE AGES

For a short while, it seemed that the Jewish religion might become the official religion of the whole Roman Empire. In the first century, many Romans were ready for a change in religion. Paganism—the worship of idols—was passing away; and large numbers of Romans were impressed by the Jewish idea that there is One God, Giver of the Law. Among the Romans who converted to Judaism were important nobles as well as common folk. Two things kept the Romans from making Jewish religion their own.

One was the revolts and rebellions of the Jews against Rome. These forced the Romans to deal harshly with the Jewish people; and the defeat of the Jewish armies caused many Romans to question whether the Jewish God was strong. (As it turned out, the Jewish people survived while the Roman Empire crumbled.)

The other was Christianity—a religion that grew out of Judaism and was begun by Jews. The Christians paid less attention to laws than the Jews did, and therefore left room for Roman laws to continue unchanged. This was important to the Romans, who were very devoted to their system of laws. And, too, Christianity made fewer demands upon the individual than the Jewish religion did.

The Christian religion spread rapidly and soon became the official religion of Rome, and the Jews of Europe remained a small minority. The Christians, however, saw the Jews as a threat and tried in every way possible to make the Jewish religion less attractive to Romans.

The Talmud Many ancient peoples faded into the vast population of the Roman Empire. The Jews did not. Though their homeland was destroyed, and the Temple was a dim memory, the Jews remained a nation. Their secret was study—the study of the Torah, and the study of the Talmud. Study reminded the Jews of their ancient Covenant, kept them loyal to their people, and helped them to survive the cruel years of Christian persecution from the fourth century on.

A coin issued in the years of the Bar Kokhba Revolt, the front depicts an ark (the Temple entrance?), the back shows a lulav (and etrog?) and an inscription in square Hebrew lettering: "First Year of Israel's Redemption."

A drawing of the Temple as imagined by an artist of the Middle Ages (from an illuminated manuscript of Maimonides' writings).

Jews in the Diaspora
from the 1st to the 5th century C.E.

- • Urban Jewish Settlements
- ■ Large Jewish Settlements
- ■ Extent of Roman Empire c.300 C.E.

Ascher

0 100 200 300 400 500 mi.

ATLANTIC OCEAN

North Sea

Baltic Sea

BRITAIN

GERMAN TRIBES

HUNS

Caspian Sea

DNIEPER R.

DON R.

DNIESTER R.

DANUBE R.

THRACE

MACEDONIA

Constantinople

Black Sea

GALATIA

HALYS R.

(ARMENIA)

PERSIAN EMPIRE

TIGRIS R.

EUPHRATES R.

Ctesiphon

Sura

Persian Gulf

ARABIA

BITHYNIA

CAPPADOCIA

CILICIA

Tarsus

Ephesus,

Antioch

SYRIA

Damascus

Nehardea

PALESTINE

Jerusalem

Ratisbon

Aquileia

Milan

Cologne

Paris

GAUL

LOIRE R.

Lyons

RHONE R.

Marseilles

ITALY

Rome

CORSICA

SARDINIA

SICILY

Salonika

GREECE

Corinth

Athens

CRETE

The Great Sea
(Mediterranean)

Cyrene

LYBIA

TRIPOLI

CYPRUS

Alexandria

Memphis

EGYPT

NILE R.

Red Sea

AFRICA

Carthage

EBRO R.

(SPAIN)

TAGUS R.

Cordova

Gades

(PORTUGAL)

The Geonim and Responsa   Not that studying the Talmud was simple. What was written had to be explained. The Talmud answered many questions, but new questions arose day by day. So the Jews of Babylonia, and the Jews of the Roman Empire turned to the great teachers who were the heads of the schools of Babylonia, the *geonim*. (*Gaon* means "excellency," and the head of each school was called a *gaon*; but the head of the school at Sura in Babylonia was called *The Gaon*.)

A building site in Spain.

With the Jewish people scattered throughout the world, answering new problems became a problem of its own. Jews far from the schools of Babylonia could read the Talmud, but not always understand it. So they used the "postal caravan" that operated from Egypt to Babylonia. They sent their questions to the geonim, and waited for a reply.

In Hebrew, this mail-order discussion is called *she'elot u-teshuvot*, but it is better known by a Latin name, *responsa* (or, singular: *responsum*). Many replies were short — sometimes only a word or two would answer a long question of law. Other replies were like brief books. For example, in the ninth century, the gaon Rav Amram sent to the Jews of Spain not only the order of the prayers as they were recited in Babylonia, but possibly the first written Jewish prayer book (see page *55*).

Reading a sermon in a 14 century Spanish synagogue.

The discussion continued up to the eleventh century when the great schools of Babylonia were broken up by persecution, and the Jews of Babylonia were forced to move to other lands. So ended one of history's greatest Jewish communities, one that had lasted nearly 2,500 years!

The Church and the Jews   In Europe, the leaders of the church became more Roman and less Jewish, even though the Christian religion had its beginnings in the Jewish religion. In 325 C.E., at the First Council of Nicaea, when all the bishops of the Roman Catholic church met together for the first time, it was decided that Christianity should break away from its Jewish past entirely. The

date of Easter, which had always been the same as that of Passover (since Jesus' Last Supper was really a Passover *seder*), was changed, and Christians were told not to eat *matzah*, to visit the synagogues, or to keep the Sabbath on the seventh day. Afterward, the Christian Sabbath was kept on Sunday.

In 339 C.E., the emperor Constantius forbade the Jews from owning Christian slaves. Many Jews had operated large farms in the Roman style, by using slaves—but, since most slaves were now Christian, these Jews were forced to give up farming.

Church leaders often tried to protect Jews from persecution, but local monks and priests taught their followers that the Jews had murdered Jesus and were the enemies of Christianity. Jewish life in the Roman Empire was made difficult by this teaching, and in the end it led to persecutions and bitter feelings.

Even into the Middle Ages, Jews continued to live in and around the Holy Land. Many were employed as dyers of fabric; and the secret of making the deep purple dye was closely guarded. In Europe the cloth was so precious that it was said that rulers were "raised to the purple."

Jews and Muslims   As the Middle Ages dawned, another new religion arose in the Middle East, Islam. It began as a warrior religion, and to this day, in many parts of the world, it remains a religion that celebrates war. In many ways, however, the world of Islam was kinder to the Jews than was the Christian world. Jews were allowed to govern themselves, to practice the Jewish religion freely, and to continue their study of Talmud and Torah. And nearly ninety percent of the Jews of the world lived under Muslim rule by the year 712 C.E.

The Age of Faith   It was an age of religion. Christians believed deeply in Christianity throughout the Middle Ages. Muslims believed deeply in Islam. And the Jews believed deeply in their Torah. For the Jews, it was belief and faith that brought them through the hard times, that gave them hope when all else was taken from them.

Jews were dyers of cloth, farmers, lenders of money, tradespeople, craftspeople, teachers, and merchants. Wherever new cities developed, Jewish merchants and tradespeople set up shop. They were so much a part of city life that Christian rulers and church leaders would often *invite* Jews to settle and trade in a new place. And wherever they went, they built synagogues, studied the Torah and the Talmud, and practiced their way of life.

Ashkenazi and Sephardi   Most of the Jews who lived in the lands of Europe north of Spain and Italy traced their beginnings back to the large Jewish community of Italy. But as they became more independent—having their own rabbis and their own practices—they began to refer to themselves as *Ashkenazi* Jews. Those Jews who lived in Spain, Italy, North Africa, and Asia came to be called *Sephardi* Jews. For a while the two communities had separate histories, each with its own set of customs. And that is how we will tell the story—beginning with the Jews of the north, then continuing with the Sephardi Jews, and then telling how the two were rejoined at the dawn of modern times.

An Ashkenazi Jewish artist of the late fourteenth century drew this picture of a Jew making *Havdalah.* In one hand, he holds the Havdalah candle and in the other, a cup of wine. (From a Vatican collection.)

UNIT ONE

THE JEWS OF ASH-KENAZ

The first Jewish communities in the Roman Empire were trading outposts. The Jews were mainly merchants and traders. Slowly, the trading posts became cities, and Jews earned their livings as shopkeepers, peddlers, tailors, tentmakers, butchers, limeburners, transporters, doctors, and poets.

They bought land for Jewish cemeteries; built synagogues; set up Jewish courts, schools, and charities. In some places they had their own small governments, as well. Though they often lived far from Rome itself, many Jews were citizens of the Roman Empire.

All this began to change as more and more Romans converted to Christianity and the church began its long campaign to take away the rights and freedoms of Rome's Jewish citizens.

2 JEWS IN CHRISTIAN KINGDOMS

The Jews in Europe   The second Temple in Jerusalem was destroyed in 70 c.e. The Jewish community in Rome was already settled. The Christian religion was just beginning to spread. And, at first, it was the Christian church and its new converts that the Roman Empire persecuted. But in 313 c.e., Emperor Constantine the Great declared Christianity equal to all other Roman religions. The persecution ended.

Constantine also moved the capitol of the empire to his new city in the east, Constantinople. And the bishop of Rome, called the *Pope* ("father"), rose to power. Rome became the center of Christianity. And the Jews of Rome, where once as many as twelve synagogues may have stood, now were ruled more by the church than by the empire.

Through the long years of the Middle Ages, the church would prove to be a cruel, almost heartless ruler. The Jews would suffer greatly.

At the same time, there were Jewish communities throughout Europe. Jewish traders and merchants lived in Paris, Toulouse, Narbonne, and Marseilles in what is now France. They lived along the Rhine and Danube rivers, in what is now Belgium, and in Greece. And their numbers were growing.

Ransoming the Captives   One reason for this growth was the rescue of Jews in trouble. Many Jews had been sold into slavery as Jewish revolts against the Roman Empire failed. Later, Jews were kidnapped by gangs or pirates and held for ransom. The Jewish communities recalled the teachings of the Torah and Talmud, and tried to save these Jews. Though they were not rich, they sent money to ransom Jews being held captive; or they bought freedom for Jewish slaves. And thus, through charity and kindness, the Jews helped one another.

Buying freedom. Whenever possible, Jewish communities raised money to trade for the freedom of Jews who had been sold into slavery.

In 1932, an ancient Jewish synagogue of the third century, C.E., was discovered at Dura Europas, on the Euphrates River. The art—such as the painting here of Ezekiel calling on the four winds to revive the dead—decorated both walls and ceiling, showing many scenes from the Bible.

To Teach the Jews   The Catholic church and the later emperors of Rome took away many of the Jews' rights of citizenship in the empire. Toward the middle of the fifth century, Emperor Theodosius II forbade the Jews to become part of the government. Christianity became the *only* official religion of the empire. In 533, Emperor Justinian I ordered that Jews stop studying Mishnah and Talmud and commentaries to the Bible. (They did not obey; and Rome's armies were busy protecting the borders, so nothing was done to force the Jews to stop studying.)

Not long after Justinian, Pope Gregory I offered money to any Jew willing to convert to Christianity. He hoped that the Jewish religion would soon disappear. He, too, ordered the Jews to stop studying. He called the Jews the worst enemy of Christianity, but he preached that they should not be harmed.

Rashi's commentary (shown below in an early manuscript) made it possible for even the simplest Jew to study the Bible and the Talmud. It became a cornerstone of Jewish education through the ages.

The Jews of Ashkenaz   Far away from Rome, a strong Jewish community grew up along the Rhine River. In the great schools of cities like Mainz and Worms, the study of Talmud continued, as it did in Babylonia. That region of what is now Germany and France was called *Ashkenaz*, and the Jews of Christian Europe came to be called the *Ashkenazim*. Jewish students from near and far came to study Talmud in the schools on the Rhine, and among them the most famous and important was the brilliant young man, Rashi.

Rashi   Rashi (a name made up of the first letters of *R*abbi *Sh*lomo ben *I*saac) was born in Troyes, France about 1040 C.E. After some years of study in the north, he returned home. He was twenty-five years old, and already people spoke of his brilliance. He started his own school; and, as time went by, his students started schools, too. Young people no longer had to travel north for their Jewish education. The schools of France were now famous.

Rashi wrote commentaries (notes) explaining nearly all the books of the Bible and the Talmud. Even today, to study Bible or Talmud seriously, one must study the works of Rashi. He had hundreds of pupils, but his best students were members of his own family. He taught his daughters to study Torah and Talmud; and all three became famous for their learning. His daughters married scholars and their children were scholars. Along with other students, his family added to the work of Rashi, explaining it and completing it. They were called the *tosafists* ("those who add"); and the work, when completed, was like a new Talmud, a Talmud of Ashkenaz.

The Crusades   In 1095, Pope Urban II called on his followers to go to Palestine to fight the Muslims. Those who answered the Pope's call put crosses on their clothing and were called "Crusaders." An army of Crusaders gathered and started marching from France to the valley of the Rhine.

Although they were bound for Jerusalem, the Crusaders were filled with anti-Jewish feelings. When they saw the wealthy Jewish communities in Germany, they paused to attack "the murderers of Christ," as they called the Jews. On May 3, 1096, ten Jews were killed by Crusaders outside the synagogue of Speyer on the French-German border. The suffering had just begun.

By the end of the First Crusade, more than 5,000 Jews had been killed in towns like Mainz, Worms, Xanten, Regensberg, Metz, and Prague. This terrible toll came in the last years of Rashi's life. Rashi died in 1105.

Crusaders. It was the cross on their costume that gave them their name.

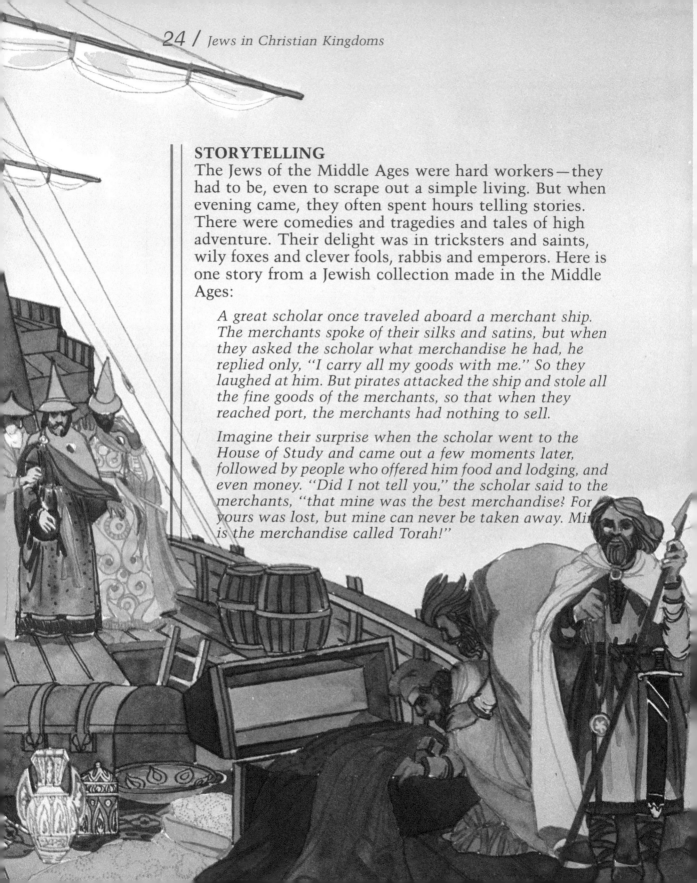

STORYTELLING

The Jews of the Middle Ages were hard workers—they had to be, even to scrape out a simple living. But when evening came, they often spent hours telling stories. There were comedies and tragedies and tales of high adventure. Their delight was in tricksters and saints, wily foxes and clever fools, rabbis and emperors. Here is one story from a Jewish collection made in the Middle Ages:

A great scholar once traveled aboard a merchant ship. The merchants spoke of their silks and satins, but when they asked the scholar what merchandise he had, he replied only, "I carry all my goods with me." So they laughed at him. But pirates attacked the ship and stole all the fine goods of the merchants, so that when they reached port, the merchants had nothing to sell.

Imagine their surprise when the scholar went to the House of Study and came out a few moments later, followed by people who offered him food and lodging, and even money. "Did I not tell you," the scholar said to the merchants, "that mine was the best merchandise? For yours was lost, but mine can never be taken away. Mine is the merchandise called Torah!"

The Crusades. The Christians glorified the Crusaders and called them heroes, but the Crusades were often little more than excuses for looting and murder.

The Later Crusades   The murderous work of the Crusades went on. The Jews of Jerusalem were massacred when the Crusaders captured the Holy City in 1099. Those not killed were sold into slavery. In 1190, the English Crusaders surrounded York and sealed up the Jewish community in the castle keep. Seeing there was no escape, Rabbi Yom Tov ben Isaac of York reminded the community that ancient rabbis like Akiba had suffered torture and death rather than give up their religion. The Jews of York chose *Kiddush ha-Shem*, "Sanctification"; they took their own lives rather than fall into the hands of the bloodthirsty Crusaders.

The period of the Crusades continued even into the fourteenth century, when the "Shepherds' Crusade," a gang of 40,000 Christians with no real leader, marched through France from north to south. Along the way, they destroyed 120 Jewish communities.

The church called Jesus "the Prince of Peace," but the Jews came to think that the Christian messiah was a prince of evil.

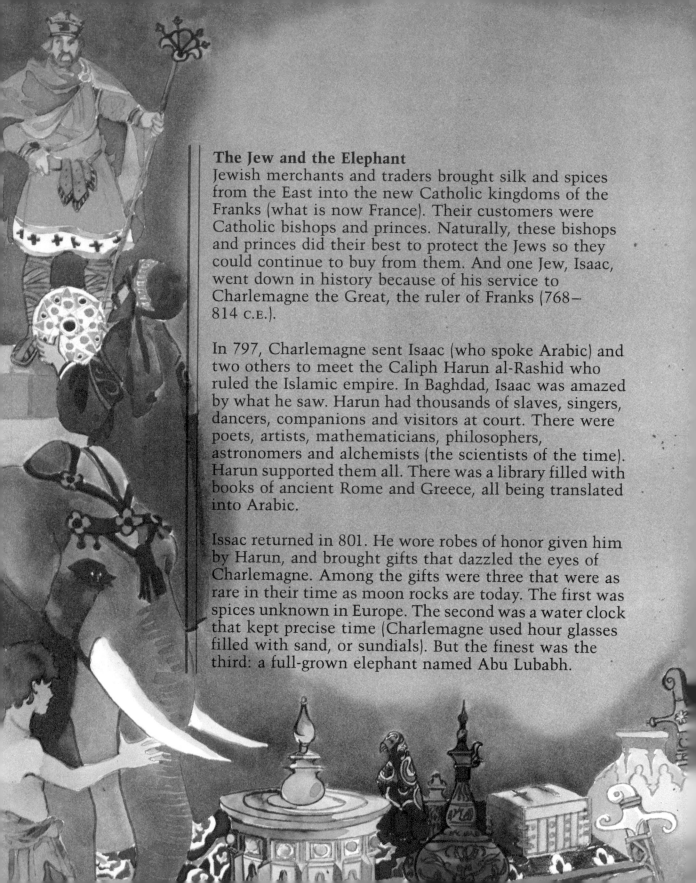

The Jew and the Elephant

Jewish merchants and traders brought silk and spices from the East into the new Catholic kingdoms of the Franks (what is now France). Their customers were Catholic bishops and princes. Naturally, these bishops and princes did their best to protect the Jews so they could continue to buy from them. And one Jew, Isaac, went down in history because of his service to Charlemagne the Great, the ruler of Franks (768–814 C.E.).

In 797, Charlemagne sent Isaac (who spoke Arabic) and two others to meet the Caliph Harun al-Rashid who ruled the Islamic empire. In Baghdad, Isaac was amazed by what he saw. Harun had thousands of slaves, singers, dancers, companions and visitors at court. There were poets, artists, mathematicians, philosophers, astronomers and alchemists (the scientists of the time). Harun supported them all. There was a library filled with books of ancient Rome and Greece, all being translated into Arabic.

Issac returned in 801. He wore robes of honor given him by Harun, and brought gifts that dazzled the eyes of Charlemagne. Among the gifts were three that were as rare in their time as moon rocks are today. The first was spices unknown in Europe. The second was a water clock that kept precise time (Charlemagne used hour glasses filled with sand, or sundials). But the finest was the third: a full-grown elephant named Abu Lubabh.

3 THE WANDERING JEWS

Christian Europe in the Middle Ages was a world filled with superstition. There were some educated men and women among the upper classes and in the service of the church, but peasants and local preachers were mainly ignorant and illiterate. Belief in demons and witches was widespread.

Blaming the Jews Local preachers blamed the Jews for every kind of evil. When the "Host"—a wafer used in Communion services—disappeared from a church (perhaps to feed hungry Christians), they said that Jews had stolen it to desecrate it (make it unfit for use in church).

The worst false teaching was the blood libel. Jews were accused of murdering Christian children to use their blood in baking Passover matzah. Anyone who knows the Jewish laws of *kashrut*, "purity," knows that blood is one thing Jews truly avoid. Educated non-Jews knew this. Popes and scholars often spoke out against this hateful foolishness. But the ignorant people listened to their local preachers.

One anti-Jewish riot followed another. In Norwich, England in 1144, a Christian boy was found dead. A monk accused the Jews of murdering the boy for his blood, and a riot followed. Jews were beaten and murdered. In 1298, the Jews of Roettingen, Germany, were said to have desecrated the Host. Twenty or more Jewish communities were attacked in revenge.

Doomed to Wander In a church council in 1215, Pope Innocent III decreed that no help should be given to Jews by princes or kings. "The Jews are doomed to wander about the earth as fugitives and vagabonds," he wrote. And he ordered that there should be a new group, the Inquisition, to seek out anyone who had pretended to convert to Christianity, but still practiced the Jewish religion or any other.

As the Black Death spread, Jews were driven from town to town. Hated and feared, they were often accused of practicing black magic and poisoning wells.

In Germany during the Black Death, Jews were forced to wander from one small kingdom to another, until finally many were driven to the east, into Poland.

The Black Death   More anti-Jewish rioting broke out in 1348 when a disease called the Black Death swept across Europe. As the plague spread from Asia to the Mediterranean Sea, from one-quarter to one-half of all the people of Europe died. The local preachers and monks blamed this, too, on the Jews. They said the Jews were causing the disease by poisoning drinking water in the wells.

Jews were tortured and forced to "confess." The false "confessions" were sent from town to town. Jews were beaten and slain in over 300 communities from Poland to Christian Spain. In Mainz, where Rashi had studied Talmud, some 6,000 Jews were killed.

Forced to Wander   Pope Innocent had ordered that Jews wear special clothing. In Vienna, they were forced to wear a strange hat. In France, they had to sew yellow badges on the front and back of their clothing. It was an idea borrowed from the Muslims. But it was just the begin-

ning of Jewish troubles. In 1182, the Jews were forced to leave the royal area of France (in and around Paris). Then, in 1198, they were allowed to return, but had to pay special taxes to the king. They had lost their freedom, too. Now they were said to be the king's "property."

In 1290, the Jews were ordered to leave England. All their property was taken by the king. Most went across the channel to France. But in 1306, the Jews were expelled again from France, and the royal treasury again took all their money and property.

Germany was not a nation. It was made up of many small kingdoms and dukedoms. As the Jews were forced to leave one kingdom, they moved to another. But, following the great slaughter at the time of the Black Death, the burning of the entire Jewish community at Strasbourg, and other persecutions, the Jews took up their packs and moved eastward, into Poland.

DISPUTATIONS: PUTTING THE TALMUD ON TRIAL

The church saw that the Jews' strength came through study. The study of Torah and Talmud kept the Jews alive to their tradition and reminded them of their covenant. So the church said that the Talmud should be placed on trial (they could not place the Torah on trial, since it is a part of the Christian Bible). A number of public trials were held, called *disputations*. Many were recorded by the church, and we can read them today.

Disputations were dangerous for the Jew who defended the Talmud. If he was too good, he was often accused of denying the truth of church teachings. The penalty for that could be death. If, on the other hand, he was not good enough, there was a chance that some Jews listening might actually think that Christianity was a better religion, and convert!

A disputation was held in Paris in 1240. King Louis IX was among the judges. The Jews of France were in fear of

A disputation between Christian and Jew.

KEEPING TORAH STUDY ALIVE

Though the Jews were forced to wander from place to place, they kept the flame of Jewish learning and study alive through these dark days. These were the years of the tosafists in France and Germany (see page 23). An early link in this chain of teaching was Rabbi Gershom of Mainz (c. 960–1028). Rashi said that all Ashkenazi Jewry depended on Gershom's teachings and that all are his students. He was called *Me'or ha-Golah*, "The Light of the Exile." Another link was Jacob Tam (1100–1171), the grandson of Rashi. He headed the academy at Champagne in France, and was so great a teacher that he was called simply *Rabbenu* ("Our Rabbi") Tam, "Our Perfect Master."

One of the greatest teachers of the Middle Ages was Rabbi Meir of Rothenburg (c. 1215–1293). He was in

The Jews of Constance come to meet Pope Martin V. They were soon to be disappointed by his words.

what might happen. Throughout the trial, they fasted and read from the Torah and Talmud. On the fourth day, the Talmud was judged to be "guilty" of being anti-Christian. Precious, handwritten copies of the Talmud were gathered from all of France, brought into the square in front of Notre Dame Cathedral, and burned. Jews stood and wept.

In 1263, the aged rabbi Nahmanides defended the Talmud in a disputation in Barcelona, Spain. The Talmud was accused of not accepting Jesus as the Messiah. Nahmanides argued that the Bible spoke of a time of peace for all that would follow the coming of the Messiah. Since Jesus had come, but peace had not, Nahmanides said, Jesus could not be the messiah spoken of in the Bible. The King of Spain was forced to declare the Talmud innocent in this case. But it was a sad victory for Nahmanides, for the king then expelled him from Spain.

Another disputation. Both Christian and Jew hold books, each quoting statements to prove his own point. Since the judges were usually Christian, the outcome was usually the same.

Paris in 1242 and saw the burning of the Talmud there. He settled in Rothenburg, in Germany. But when Emperor Rudolph I ordered that the Jews pay heavy taxes, he led many of his community to Italy, hoping to escape persecution there. Rudolph sent agents to Italy to kidnap Meir, and he was thrown into prison in Germany. Then Rudolph announced that he would free Rabbi Meir in exchange for 20,000 marks of silver.

Rabbi Meir's followers took up a collection and raised the money, but when Meir heard he sent word to stop them from paying. He was sure that if Rudolph was paid his ransom, he would just kidnap other Jews and ask for more ransom money. So Rabbi Meir chose to stay in prison for the last seven years of his life, writing commentaries and prayers, some of which we still recite in our synagogues today.

Pope Martin V (1417) told the Jews, "You have the Law, but do not understand it. The old has passed away and the new been found." Such was the attitude of the Catholic Church.

Poland   There were small groups of Jews living in Poland in the eleventh and twelfth centuries. They probably came as traders and merchants, setting up outposts in the important trade between the eastern and western nations. But most Jews came to Poland from Germany in the thirteenth century—and by invitation!

In the 1240s, fierce tribes of Mongols from the Far East invaded Poland, looting and destroying. Afterward, the rulers of Poland wished to resettle their cities and build up trade and business. In 1264 Boleslav the Pious, prince of Kalisz in Poland, issued an invitation to the Jewish city-dwellers of Germany. It was a charter: Boleslav promised to protect the Jews if they would come to Kalisz and help build up its commerce. King Casimir the Great widened this charter to cover the whole kingdom of Poland. Jews came by the thousands.

In Poland, the Jews became collectors of taxes, merchants, craftspeople, and bankers. Some leased land from the Polish nobles and watched over farming, milling, and the harvesting of trees. Many became managers of large Polish estates. By 1500, there were about 15,000 Jews in Poland; and by 1648 there were about 150,000.

The New Academies   The old schools of Talmud learning along the Rhine had been destroyed by the Crusaders and other persecutions. But as one Jewish saying goes, "Torah is the best merchandise," because it travels anywhere without spoiling. Now, new and greater *yeshivot* ("academies") arose in cities like Prague and Vilna. To these yeshivot hundreds of students from all over Poland and Lithuania came to study with famous masters. Some students spent their entire lifetimes debating and discussing Jewish ideas and questions of Jewish law. In return, they were honored and respected by the whole Jewish community. And Poland became a center of Jewish learning for some 500 years!

4 MYSTICISM AND MESSIAHS

Jewish Mysticism For the Jews of Ashkenaz, the Middle Ages were difficult and dangerous. Faced by the evils of the world, many Jews became superstitious as their Christian neighbors. One rabbi taught that a child should not be allowed to see "a dog or a Christian" on the way to his first day in school. If he did, the rabbi said, he would never be a great scholar.

Mysticism is something far more serious. One who practices mysticism, a mystic, tries to enter into God's world, to become almost a part of God. Jewish mystics tried to reach these heights mainly through long hours of study and many days of fasting. They tried to see God's world as a place of beauty and holiness. Surely that was a worthwhile goal in these hard times.

Mystical teachings
are passed from
teacher to teacher.

Hasidei Ashkenaz   Mysticism came to the Jews of Germany, France, and Christian Spain through the teachings of a few Jews called the *Hasidei Ashkenaz* (the "pious" or "religious ones" of Ashkenaz). The leaders of this group combined their mystical studies with careful attention to the commandments of the Torah. The family of Kalonymus were the best known leaders, and the most famous of all was Judah he-Hasid (Judah "the Pious," c. 1150–1217). He was the main author of the *Sefer Hasidim* ("Book of the Pious") which taught how a Jew could live righteously, "in the image of God."

The mystical teachings of the Hasidei Ashkenaz were never widely studied. They were passed on from teacher to student in small groups, and slowly spread southward into France and Christian Spain. But the teachings of righteousness, of living according to the ancient covenant, became very popular. And, though the Hasidei Ashkenaz were never a large group, their ideas gave new hope to many of the Jews of France and Germany—new hope in a time of great suffering.

The Kabbalah   The chain of teaching of the mystics came to be known as the *Kabbalah* ("Tradition"). The basic ideas of this secret "Tradition" were first recorded in a book called the *Bahir*, "Brightness," near the end of the twelfth century in Provence, France. The *Bahir* tells of *sefirot*, levels of knowing God. It speaks of the inner universe, the world of the spirit, as being like an onion—as one level is understood and peeled away, you find another level beneath. And as you understand that level and peel it away, there is yet another level. A Jewish mystic did not think it possible ever to know God completely, but found beauty and joy in discovering more and more about the divine mystery.

From Provence, these teachings spread further south to Christian Spain, especially to the town of Gerona. There, it was taught by the famous rabbi Nahmanides in the thir-

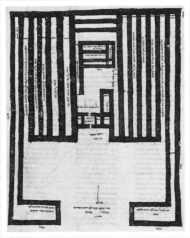

teenth century. Because of his fame, the teachings became more popular and more widespread. The stage was set for the most important of all Jewish mystical works, the "Talmud" of mysticism.

The Zohar   Mysticism was not new to Judaism. Some of the rabbis of the Talmud had been mystics. And the Talmud warned that mysticism could be dangerous if one were not prepared for it. The Talmud said that mysticism should not be studied until a person reached the age of forty, that it should only be studied in very small groups, and that only the greatest of scholars should pratice reaching God's hidden world. Among the great rabbis of the Talmud who were mystics were Akiba and also Rabbi Simeon bar Yohai.

Left: A calendar for the year 1276, showing the moon (Hebrew) calculations in the center, and the sun's year around the outside. Right, top: This mystic art shows the word "mitzvah" becoming "mitzvot" (you'll have to look closely) through the ten *spheres* by which God controls the world. Right, bottom: a diagram of the ancient Temple gives the idea that we can all find a path to the Holy of Holies.

Toward the end of the thirteenth century, in Christian Spain, a man named Moses de Leon "discovered" (in truth, he probably wrote much of) a many-volumed book called the *Zohar,* "Brilliance." Moses de Leon claimed that the Zohar was written in the days of the Talmud by Rabbi Simeon. He said that Simeon wrote it when he was forced to spend long years hidden in a cave studying when the Romans forbade the Jews to study Torah.

The Zohar is a commentary on the Torah, but it is full of difficult, mystical teachings and strange legends. Through the years it became the basic textbook for Jewish mystics; and, one of the most studied books in Jewish life.

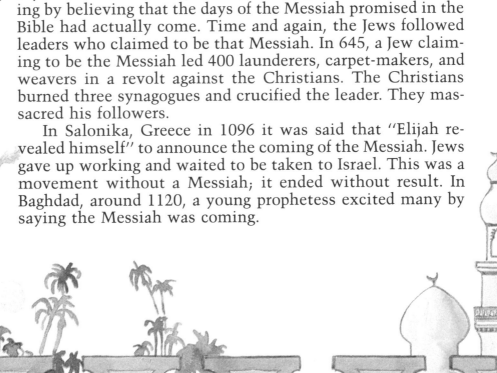

A young Jewish prophetess in Baghdad predicts the coming of the Messiah.

The False Messiahs While Jewish mystics turned inward, other Jews sought relief from suffering by believing that the days of the Messiah promised in the Bible had actually come. Time and again, the Jews followed leaders who claimed to be that Messiah. In 645, a Jew claiming to be the Messiah led 400 launderers, carpet-makers, and weavers in a revolt against the Christians. The Christians burned three synagogues and crucified the leader. They massacred his followers.

In Salonika, Greece in 1096 it was said that "Elijah revealed himself" to announce the coming of the Messiah. Jews gave up working and waited to be taken to Israel. This was a movement without a Messiah; it ended without result. In Baghdad, around 1120, a young prophetess excited many by saying the Messiah was coming.

About 1172, a Jew in Yemen proclaimed himself Messiah. He told rich Jews to give away everything they owned to prepare for the End of Days. Maimonides (see chapter 7) wrote to the leaders of Yemen that this request was ridiculous. If the rich gave their money to the poor, the rich would be poor, and the formerly poor would have to give all their money to the formerly rich—money would be passed back and forth forever. The solution? Maimonides suggested that the leaders of Yemenite Jewry either banish the man or put him to death.

But false Messiahs continued to appear whenever suffering or world events caused unrest among the Jews; and there were always those ready to follow, so strong was their belief that God would save the people of Israel. In truth, looking forward to a peaceful, loving world—the promise of the days of the messiah—is part of being Jewish. Without this hope for the future, we could hardly take the kind of pride in our people, or ourselves, that we do.

IDEAS FROM THE ZOHAR

A word once spoken goes up to Heaven, and prepares for the speaker good or evil as a portion in the World to Come.

A woman is like a candle lit by another. As two candles give forth the same light, so is the light of the husband and the wife the same.

The person who toils in Torah and discovers in it new meanings that are true, contributes new Torah which is treasured by the Jews.

The Sabbath is scented with the perfume of Paradise, and as it reaches earth sorrow and sighing flee away, and peace and joy reign supreme.

5 GHETTO AND SHTETL

For hundreds of years, the Jews of Ashkenaz lived set off from non-Jews. By the end of the sixteenth century, Ashkenazi Jews had two different kinds of communities—the ghetto and the shtetl. Both grew out of the Jewish custom of living closely together: in Jewish "quarters" or neighborhoods in the cities; and in their own small villages in the countryside. Some Jewish communities even built walls around their section of town to keep out thieves and rioters. But the church and the governments saw another purpose for such walls: to lock Jews in.

The Age of the Ghetto In 1516, the church ordered that walls be built around the Jewish Quarter of Venice. From that time on, all Jews in Venice had to live within these walls. It happened that the Jewish Quarter was near a foundry where cannons were made. So it was given the name *ghetto*, meaning "foundry." The gates were closed each night; the Jews were locked in until daybreak. The idea, and the name ghetto, spread.

Soon there were ghettos all over Europe; and, too, other forms of persecution. Jews were sometimes forced to wear badges on their clothing. They were not allowed to own land, to join crafts guilds, or to do the kinds of work Christians did. For many years, copies of the Talmud were gathered and burned publicly. Jewish communities were taxed heavily and the Jews were plagued by poverty. Disputations were held; and Jews were forced to listen to long sermons.

The ghettos forced the Jews to create stronger communities. In fact, life inside the ghetto seemed better to most Jews than life outside! Among Christians, rich and poor were in entirely separate worlds. Inside the ghetto, the rich helped the poor—and even the poorest Jew was treated decently, for such was the decree of Jewish law.

Most Jews lived in crowded houses, in the cramped spaces of the ghettos, yet they worked together, studied together,

Ghettos might be beautiful, but the guards, the walls, and the gates that closed at night were reminders of their true purpose.

The invention of printing by movable type in the 15th century made it possible for Jews to own copies of prayerbooks, Bibles, commentaries—even the Talmud.

JEWS IN THE RENAISSANCE

Isaac Abrabanel left Spain in 1492 when Jews were forced to emigrate. He arrived in Venice, Italy in 1503 to find himself in the middle of an explosion of human energy. It was the time of the Renaissance. Christians were rediscovering the works of Greek and Latin writers; freeing themselves of the church; creating new sculpture, poetry, and art. And many were interested in ancient Hebrew writings, too. Isaac's son, Judah, became famous for a book that told of how the universe could be loved. Jews were invited to impart their knowledge to Christian scholars. Italy became the great early center of Hebrew printing (the Talmud in the form we know it today was designed and printed for the first time in Italy during the Renaissance). Jewish composers wrote new Jewish music for the synagogue in Renaissance style, and rabbis commented on the Torah, using Renaissance ideas.

During the Renaissance, some Jews even tried to look at the Jewish past with new eyes. The finest of these thinkers was Azariah dei Rossi (c. 1511 – 1578) who studied Greek literature only to discover the works of Josephus and Philo (see Volume I), Jewish thinkers who had been all but forgotten. He also studied the Talmud in a very modern way, saying that the legends were not historical and that the Jewish calendar was a late invention created by the rabbis of the Talmud. Because of his opinions, his book was banned by the rabbis of his time, and it was many years before his pioneering work was understood.

The Renaissance never became a Jewish Renaissance. It was too full of Christian thought. And the period came to an end before the Jews outside of Italy were freed from the ghettos and shtetls to become a part of the new world the Renaissance helped to create.

celebrated together, prayed together, and tried to make life worthwhile.

The Shtetl   It was also in the sixteenth century that the *shtetl* (Yiddish for "little town") began to take shape. Shtetls grew up in Eastern Europe, especially in Poland and Lithuania, where the Jews settled outside the main cities, in the countryside. A shtetl had no walls; no gates that could be locked. And shtetls often were protected by the government since many Jews served the Polish nobles as bankers, tax collectors, and farm managers.

The shtetl was a Jewish community. At its center stood the synagogue; and at the center of the life of the synagogue was the rabbi. Being rich was nice, but being a good student was thought even more worthy. Most were poor, but all gave charity, *tzedakah*. It was said that even the poorest Jew could find someone poorer to help. Love, warmth, and friendship were found among families, relatives, and neighbors.

Shtetl and Ghetto   In both shtetl and ghetto, the Jews had their own town councils, collected their own taxes, ran their own schools, their own courts of law, and their own burial societies. The official holidays of the shtetl and ghetto were the Jewish holidays; and, among these, Shabbat, the day of rest, was the most welcome.

An eighteenth century Polish synagogue.

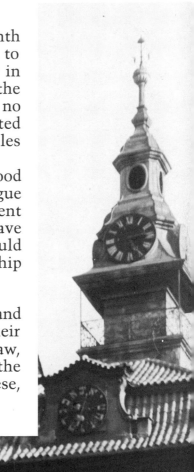

In Prague's ghetto, the central building had two clocks—the Hebrew one ran backwards!

SHULHAN ARUCH

Since ancient times, Jewish laws had been made in the Talmud, in responsa, and in *takkanot*, "rulings" of great rabbis. Finding the answer to a question of law was difficult. This led to the writing of codes or collections of the law. Some were just lists, others were filled with commentary. The most famous was written by Joseph Caro (1488–1575) of Tzfat (Safed). It was called the *Shulhan Aruch*, the "Set Table." From the moment it was printed in Venice in 1565, it became the guidebook for Sephardi Jewry.

Caro was Sephardi and had recorded only the Sephardi customs. But his admirer, Moses Isserles (1530?–1572) added a commentary to the Shulhan Aruch that included all the Ashkenazi customs. Slowly, over the next hundred years, the Shulhan Aruch and Isserles' commentary, which he called *Ha-Mappah*, the "Tablecloth," became the standard codes of Jewish laws for Jews around the world.

THE COUNCIL OF THE FOUR LANDS

Each shtetl in Poland and Lithuania had its own small government. By the middle of the sixteenth century, a national "Jewish government" was set up, too. This was called the *Va'ad Arba Aratzot*, the "Council of the Four Lands." (The four "lands" were Greater Poland, Lesser Poland, Volhynia, and Lithuania.) The Council was made up of the leading Jews from shtetls and cities throughout the lands. It met usually twice a year during important fairs. It governed the collection of taxes, settled arguments between provinces, watched over the schools and yeshivot, and directed religious life. For almost 200 years, it served the Jewish communities, and along with the great yeshivot made Polish Jewry the crown jewel of all Jewish communities in the world.

From time to time rioting broke out against the Jews. The woodcut above is of a riot that took place in Frankfurt-am-Main in 1614.

Life was lived according to the laws of Talmud. But, since most Jews could not study Talmud from start to finish, the laws that were scattered throughout this great work were collected and arranged into guidebooks, codes. As time went on, these codes became more and more complete, ruling everyday life from morning to night.

Problems   Jewish life was now more orderly and regular, but still there were problems. Food and money were often scarce. Shtetls and ghettos were sometimes invaded by Christian mobs calling the Jews "Christ-killers" and looting, burning, and murdering. Fire was fearsome because the small, wooden homes were built close together and wood was burned in the winter to keep the houses warm. When a fire broke out, it was not usually one building that burned, but a whole street, or a whole town.

The Jews learned to rebuild after the fires; and to clean up after the raiding Christians left. Life went on. And, though they sometimes wondered why they suffered so much, they felt a special nearness to God.

THE JEWS OF SEPHARAD

We have seen how the Jews of Ashkenaz lived from the time of the destruction of the Second Temple to the middle of the seventeenth century. Despite the hardships they suffered, the Jews of Ashkenaz remained true to their faith, continued and enlarged upon the study of Bible and Talmud, and continually practiced the Jewish way of life. The great yeshivahs of Germany had led to the great academies of

France, and this tradition was inherited by the Jews of Eastern Europe. The Jews in the north were never truly separated from the Jews who lived in the lands from India to Africa and Spain, the Sephardi Jews; and from time to time what happened in the lands of the Sephardi Jews became important even to the north. So it was in the case of the *Zohar* and, later, the *Shulhan Aruch*; and we shall see other cases as we go on with our story.

During many of these 1,600 years, the Jews of Ashkenaz were the minority of the Jews in the world. The Jews of *Sepharad* were much more numerous. Just as the Jews in the north traced their beginnings to the Jewish communities in Italy after the destruction of the Temple; the Jews in Sepharad traced their beginnings to the great community of Babylonia. And, just as the Jews in the north had to contend with the Christian church which had grown out of the Jewish religion, so, too, the Jews of Sepharad had to contend with another of the "daughter" religions of Judaism—Islam.

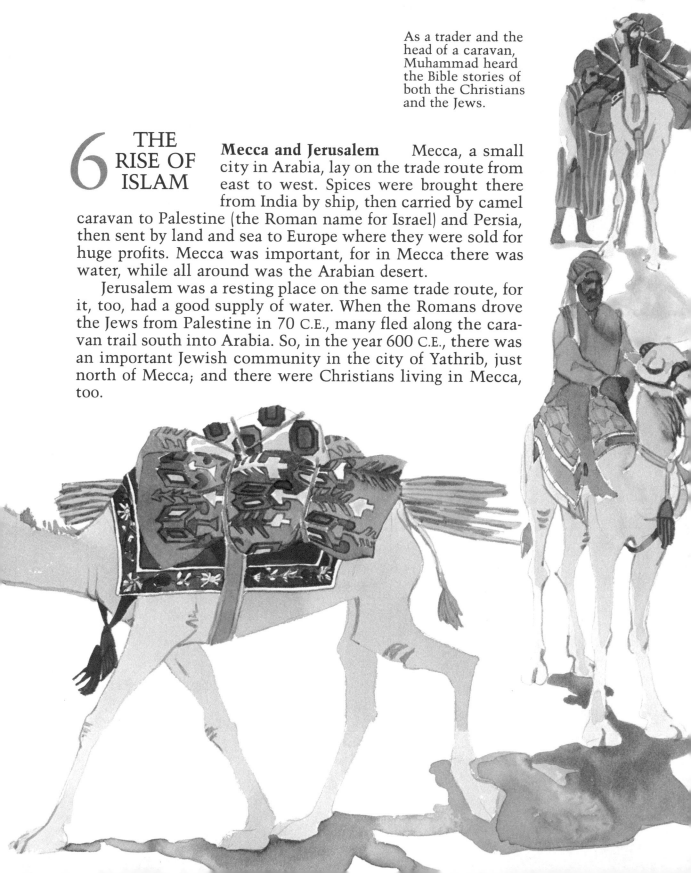

As a trader and the head of a caravan, Muhammad heard the Bible stories of both the Christians and the Jews.

6 THE RISE OF ISLAM

Mecca and Jerusalem   Mecca, a small city in Arabia, lay on the trade route from east to west. Spices were brought there from India by ship, then carried by camel caravan to Palestine (the Roman name for Israel) and Persia, then sent by land and sea to Europe where they were sold for huge profits. Mecca was important, for in Mecca there was water, while all around was the Arabian desert.

Jerusalem was a resting place on the same trade route, for it, too, had a good supply of water. When the Romans drove the Jews from Palestine in 70 C.E., many fled along the caravan trail south into Arabia. So, in the year 600 C.E., there was an important Jewish community in the city of Yathrib, just north of Mecca; and there were Christians living in Mecca, too.

Muhammad, Prophet of Allah   Now there lived in Mecca a wealthy merchant named Muhammad. Leading his caravans, he met many Jews and Christians. He saw that religion brought strength and unity to both Jews and Christians, and he began to wish for a time when the warring tribes of Arabia would share one belief and one religion. Then Muhammad dreamed that the angel Gabriel came to speak with him; and Muhammad began to call himself a prophet.

He told his followers that he was the last of the prophets, the "seal" or end of prophecy; and that his was the true message of the One God. The name of this God, he said, was *Allah* (the same as the Hebrew name for God, *Elohem*, or *Elohim*). Before him in the line of prophets, Muhammad taught, were Adam, Noah, Abraham, Moses, Solomon, and Jesus. Allah had spoken to these men, and now to Muhammad. "There is no God but Allah," he taught, "and Muhammad is his prophet."

Islam   As the number of his followers grew, Muhammad taught them stories from the Bible mixed with his personal dreams and visions. His students later collected these stories in a book called the *Koran*, which became their "Bible." Muhammad called his new religion *Islam*, "obedience" to God. It was much like Judaism.

Muslims (believers in Islam) believe that there is one God. They believe that prayer is important (they pray five times each day). They believe that fasting (not eating or drinking) is a kind of prayer. They believe in giving charity. And, they believe in making pilgrimages to their holy places. These beliefs are known as the Five Pillars of Islam.

In addition, Muhammad taught that Muslims should pray in a *mosque*, a building much like the synagogue; that they should set aside one day of rest each week (he finally settled on Friday); and that when they pray, they should face the holy city of Jerusalem.

The synagogues of the Sephardi Jews often resembled the mosques of their Muslim neighbors.

One Hundred Years of Conquest

Gathering an army, Muhammad declared war on idolatry. His followers captured Mecca and destroyed the hundreds of idols that were worshiped there. Soon they conquered all of Arabia. By the time Muhammad died, in 632, he was the ruler of a vast Arab nation.

The Arabs were glad to fight for Allah. Muhammad promised that they would become rich if they won their battles. And he promised that all who died fighting would awake in a heaven filled with special delights for the warrior. Strong and mighty, his armies won battle after battle. They put to death all who would not accept Islam — sparing only Christians and Jews since they, too, worshiped the One God. In time, they built an empire as large as any the world had ever known. It stretched from the borders of India and China across North Africa and into Spain. Indeed, when the Muslim advance was halted 100 years later, in 732, the armies were only 150 miles from the city of Paris, France.

The Western World 800 C.E.

ATLANTIC OCEAN

Legend:
- The Umayyad Caliphate of Spain
- The Byzantine (East Roman) Empire
- The Frankish (Carolingian) Empire
- Territory controlled by the Khazars
- The Abbasid Caliphate

0   100   200   400   600 miles

Arabian Sea

PERSIA

Persian Gulf

YEMEN

Mecca

Red Sea

Baghdad

Harran

EUPHRATES R.

TIGRIS R.

Antioch

Damascus

Jerusalem

Cairo

Alexandria

EGYPT

Caspian Sea

VOLGA R.

DON R.

DNIEPER R.

Black Sea

Constantinople

The Great Sea (Mediterranean)

AFRICA

LITHUANIA

Baltic Sea

POLAND

VISTULA R.

DANUBE R.

GERMANY

Cologne

Mainz

RHINE R.

FRANCE

Aachen

Saragossa

SPAIN

Toledo

Cordoba

Tangier

Fez

MUHAMMAD AND THE JEWS

At first Muhammad admired the Jews, naming them the "people of the Book." But the Jews refused to believe that he was a prophet. In his anger, Muhammad commanded that prayers be said while facing Mecca instead of Jerusalem. And when he became ruler of Yathrib (now called Medina), he ordered that the Jewish men of the city be put to death; and he made the women and children slaves.

Even so, Muhammad died believing that all Jews would one day be Muslims. He taught that Jews and Christians were special, peoples to whom Allah had once spoken. So, while the Muslims forced Jews and Christians to pay special taxes, they allowed them much freedom. Under Muslim rule, the Jews began to write in Arabic (as before they had written in Aramaic); they became doctors, merchants, poets, philsophers, and even soldiers. They often served in the government. All this in a time when the Ashkenazi Jews lived in fear of their Christian neighbors and were being persecuted continually.

The Dome of the Rock, also called the Mosque of Omar, was built by the Muslims on the spot where the ancient Jewish Temple once stood.

Among the stories Muhammed told his followers was the tale of a night journey to Jerusalem, where he rested before rising up to "the seventh heaven." Because of this story, Jerusalem became sacred to the Muslims, as it already was to Christians and Jews.

7 THE PARTNER-SHIP

The Jews in Spain   Jews first settled in Spain in the late fourth and early fifth centuries, living peacefully throughout the land. But in the fifth century, a Germanic tribe called the Visigoths conquered Spain and converted the Spanish peoples to Christianity. Here, as in Christian northern Europe, the rulers were unsure of what to do about the Jews. One Visigoth king would demand that the Jews convert to Christianity, while the next would allow them to practice their Jewish religion freely.

This back and forth of converting and not converting had a special effect on the Jews of Spain. In the end, there grew up a tradition of pretending to convert to Christianity while practicing Judaism secretly.

In 694, the Visigoth king Egica accused the Jews of trying to help the Muslim armies cross the sea to attack Europe. He declared that all Jews were now slaves. He outlawed the Jewish religion. Those Jews who could, escaped. Others were taken captive and their children were brought up as Christians. No doubt the Jews of Spain really did hope that the Muslim armies would soon cross the Straits of Gibraltar to conquer Spain.

And, in 711, the Muslims came, conquering city after city. They fought against the Christians, but they knew that the Jews of Spain could be trusted to help them. So, as each city was taken, the Muslims called the "secret" Jews out of hiding. They offered to protect the Jews, if the Jews would help them. In many places, they allowed the Jews to govern cities so that the Muslim armies could continue fighting to the north. So it happened in cities like Cordoba, Granada, Toledo, and Seville. Jews were able to practice their religion openly again, and to take part in Muslim society. And Jewish culture began to prosper.

Cordoba—The Capital   For many years, Cordoba was the most important of the Spanish cities. For the Muslims, it was the capital of Spain; and it became a

Family life in the courtyard of a Jewish home in Muslim Spain.

Outside and inside, the El Transito Synagogue, in Toledo, looked like any fourteenth century Spanish building—except for the Hebrew inscriptions and the ark that marked it as a Jewish house of worship.

center both of Arabic and Jewish learning. In 929, a Jew named Hisdai Ibn Shaprut was appointed head of the Jewish community of all Spain. Until this time, when a question of Jewish law arose, letters were sent to Babylonia. It would take months before the answers came. Hisdai saw that the new Spanish Jewish community was greater even than the community in Babylonia. So he brought a rabbi from Italy to the academy at Cordoba; and now the Jews of Spain settled questions of Jewish law for themselves.

In and around Cordoba, the Jews were farmers and physicians, in business and crafts (Hisdai himself was a physician—it was common in those days for a physician to go into government). There were great Jewish thinkers in Cordoba who studied Hebrew language and grammar, Talmud, and even the art of geography.

Spanish Jewish Culture Throughout Spain, the Jews combined their religious life with a daily life among the Muslims. They studied Jewish texts side by side with poetry and mathematics. Sometimes, all of these interests came together in the life of one person. Such a person was Samuel Ibn Nagrela.

Samuel left Cordoba in 1013 when it was invaded by an army of the Berber tribe. He settled in Granada where he later became the Vizier or ruler of the city, and general of the Muslim armies. Through twenty long years of battles, he led the Arab troops from victory to victory. At the same time, he wrote an introduction to the Talmud, composed poetry in Hebrew (though he spoke Arabic day by day), and sent money to the poor Jews of Palestine. The Jews of Spains called him Samuel Ha-Nagid, Samuel "the Prince."

Centers of Talmud study were established in Lucena and in Barcelona. To these academies came students from all over Spain. The teaching and study of Judaism became the pride of the Spanish Jewish community.

A BOOK SENT TO SPAIN; MANY BOOKS FROM SPAIN

In the ninth century, the Spanish Jews of Lucena and Barcelona wrote to the leader of Babylonian Jewry asking for help. The Spanish scholars could study Talmud and Bible, but the prayers had not been written down. They were passed on by word of mouth from one generation to the next. How could the Spanish Jews be sure that their prayer service was the same as that used in Babylonia?

An answer came from Rav Amram. He set down the order of the prayers—the *Shema,* the *Tefillah* or central blessings and the rest. It was the first written Jewish prayer book that we know of; and it was given the name *Siddur,* meaning "order." The Jews of Spain began adding to this Siddur. Their greatest poets—Solomon Ibn Gabirol, Judah Halevi, Moses Ibn Ezra—wrote new poems for the prayer book.

Ibn Ezra also wrote drinking songs (the popular music of his time); Judah Halevi composed poetry about the Holy Land. "My heart," he wrote in one poem, "is in the East, while I am in the West." Judah longed for Zion and finally left on the difficult journey to Israel. He never returned. Jewish legend tells that Halevi reached Jerusalem and was murdered as he knelt before the Western Wall, which was all that remained of the ancient Temple. Gabirol was both a poet and a philosopher. His major work, *The Fountain of Life,* was important to all of medieval philosophy. For hundreds of years it was studied in its Latin translation by Christians who thought that its author had been either Muslim or Christian. And another Spanish Jewish philosopher whose work is still studied today was Bahya ibn Paquda. In his book, *The Duties of the Heart,* Ibn Paquda reminded the Spanish Jews of the Jewish tradition of righteousness and kindness to other human beings.

Maimonides   Surprisingly, the most important of all Spanish Jews lived most of his life outside Spain. He was Moses ben Maimon, known as Maimonides (Greek for "son of Maimon") and Rambam (from the first letters of *R*abbi *M*oses *b*en *M*aimon). Moses was just thirteen years old when his family was forced to flee from Cordoba by a fierce group of Muslim warriors called the Almohades. As his family moved slowly across North Africa, Moses studied; and when the family settled in Fostat, Egypt—a few miles from Cairo—Moses became a physician. Among his patients was a very famous Muslim, the sultan Saladin the Magnificent.

But Moses did more than practice medicine. To assist the Jews of his time to follow Jewish law correctly he studied the entire Talmud and brought together a simplified code book of laws, the *Mishneh Torah* (the "Repeating of the [Oral] Torah").

In Arabic, Maimonides wrote a book giving Jewish answers to the questions of Islamic philosophers. He called this *The Guide to the Perplexed*, that is, the guide to those who

Maimonides, the physician, tending to the family of the Sultan in Cairo.

wondered how Jewish thinking and the thinking of the Muslims could both be true.

When there were troubles in the distant Jewish community of Yemen, the leaders wrote to Maimonides asking for help. He sent them a long letter of reply, including in it wisdom, guidance, and comfort. Closer at hand, he was the leader of his own Jewish community, studying Torah and Talmud with them each Sabbath. In addition, he wrote ten books on medicine; a book explaining the Jewish calendar; a book on astrology, the false science of predicting the future by the stars; and an introduction to the well-known book of Mishnah called *Pirke Avot.*

Like so many of the great Jews of Muslim Spain, Maimonides was able to live in both the Jewish and the non-Jewish worlds. Though this partnership between the Arabs and the Jews was nearing its end, it had given rise to some of the finest works of Jewish culture since the completion of the Babylonian Talmud. It was an age of splendor and genius, and many have called it the "Golden Age" of Spain.

Maimonides, the scholar, answering questions from communities as far away as Yemen on the Gulf of Arabia.

The Khazars

In most periods of Jewish history, Jews have discouraged non-Jews from converting. Rabbis explained the difficulties of Jewish law and the dangers of persecution. Converts were accepted as Jews only after a long period of study.

At some times, however, Jews have actually tried to convert non-Jews. In the early eighth century, Jewish merchants discovered an independent kingdom of Turks called the Khazars. From the facts we have, it appears that the merchants convinced the Khazar rulers to become Jewish and for almost 200 years there was a Jewish kingdom in the area. The tale of the conversion of the Khazars spread to Spain where Judah Halevi heard of it.

Halevi used the story as the dramatic setting for his book on Jewish philosophy called *Sefer ha Kuzari* ("The Book of the Khazars"). In it, a Khazar king calls upon a Greek philosopher, a Christian, a Muslim, and—finally—a Jew, to explain their religions. In the end, the king sees the wisdom of the Jewish faith and converts to it. Halevi's book taught the Jewish faith in a simple and colorful way and became popular reading among the Jews of Spain.

8 INQUISITION AND EXPULSION

The Reconquest   The partnership between Arabs and Jews in Spain came to an end for two reasons. First, fierce Arab warriors called the Almohades tried to convert the Jews of Spain to Islam by force. Second, the Christians of northern Spain gathered new armies and slowly began the reconquest of Spain.

For a while it seemed there might be a partnership between the Jews and the Christians. Many Christian rulers had Jewish advisors and appointed Jewish governors. But by the middle of the thirteenth century, only the province of Granada remained a Muslim state. The Christian government grew stronger and so did the church; and once more the Jews began to feel the heavy foot of the Catholic church upon their necks.

The Inquisition   Once again Jews were told to accept Christianity or die. Once again, many became "secret" Jews, pretending to convert while continuing to practice the Jewish religion secretly. Christians called these false converts secret Jews; Jews called them *Marranos*, the Spanish word for "swine." But in later years, the term Marrano came to be a badge of honor, for these secret Jews loyally practiced their faith and continued their secret Jewish ways for hundreds of years.

In many parts of Spain Jews still worked for kings, farmed the land, operated businesses, and wrote poetry. But for years there were scattered church persecutions against the Jews. In 1483 a committee of churchmen called the Inquisition fell into the hands of one of history's most terrible villains, Tomas de Torquemada. He led the search for unfaithful Christians, including those secretly practicing Judaism. In just twelve years, the Inquisition tortured, burned, and murdered no fewer than 13,000 "Christians"—men, women, and children—most of them Marranos.

The Inquisition sought out false converts, among them Jews who pretended to be Christians. When they were found, they were beaten and tortured, then put to death in public. This was the *auto-de-fe*, in which Jews were stripped and burned at the stake.

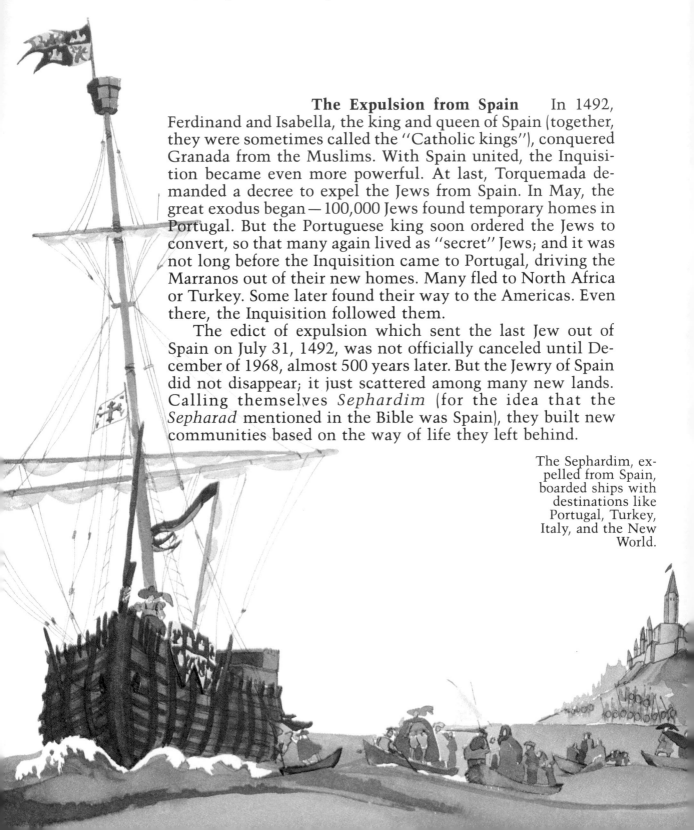

The Expulsion from Spain   In 1492, Ferdinand and Isabella, the king and queen of Spain (together, they were sometimes called the "Catholic kings"), conquered Granada from the Muslims. With Spain united, the Inquisition became even more powerful. At last, Torquemada demanded a decree to expel the Jews from Spain. In May, the great exodus began — 100,000 Jews found temporary homes in Portugal. But the Portuguese king soon ordered the Jews to convert, so that many again lived as "secret" Jews; and it was not long before the Inquisition came to Portugal, driving the Marranos out of their new homes. Many fled to North Africa or Turkey. Some later found their way to the Americas. Even there, the Inquisition followed them.

The edict of expulsion which sent the last Jew out of Spain on July 31, 1492, was not officially canceled until December of 1968, almost 500 years later. But the Jewry of Spain did not disappear; it just scattered among many new lands. Calling themselves *Sephardim* (for the idea that the *Sepharad* mentioned in the Bible was Spain), they built new communities based on the way of life they left behind.

The Sephardim, expelled from Spain, boarded ships with destinations like Portugal, Turkey, Italy, and the New World.

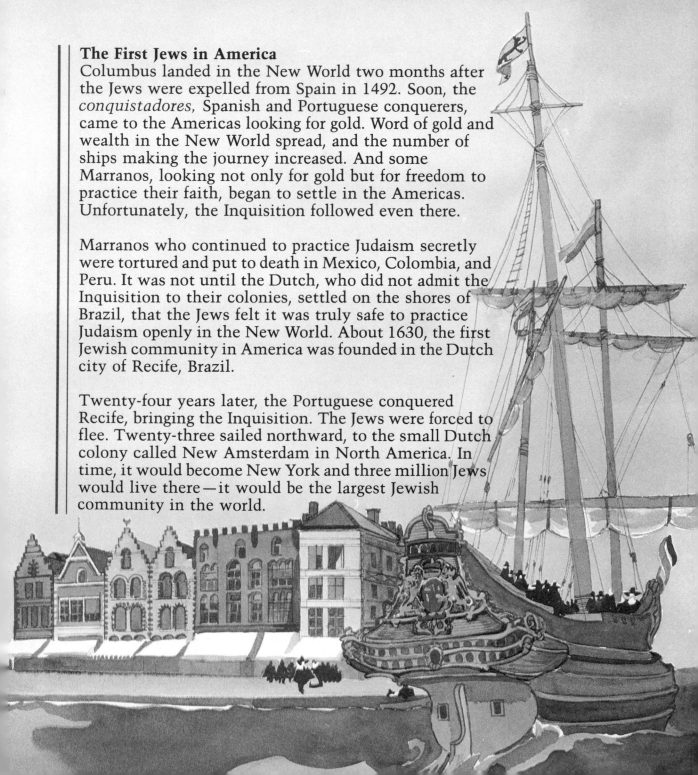

The First Jews in America

Columbus landed in the New World two months after the Jews were expelled from Spain in 1492. Soon, the *conquistadores*, Spanish and Portuguese conquerers, came to the Americas looking for gold. Word of gold and wealth in the New World spread, and the number of ships making the journey increased. And some Marranos, looking not only for gold but for freedom to practice their faith, began to settle in the Americas. Unfortunately, the Inquisition followed even there.

Marranos who continued to practice Judaism secretly were tortured and put to death in Mexico, Colombia, and Peru. It was not until the Dutch, who did not admit the Inquisition to their colonies, settled on the shores of Brazil, that the Jews felt it was truly safe to practice Judaism openly in the New World. About 1630, the first Jewish community in America was founded in the Dutch city of Recife, Brazil.

Twenty-four years later, the Portuguese conquered Recife, bringing the Inquisition. The Jews were forced to flee. Twenty-three sailed northward, to the small Dutch colony called New Amsterdam in North America. In time, it would become New York and three million Jews would live there—it would be the largest Jewish community in the world.

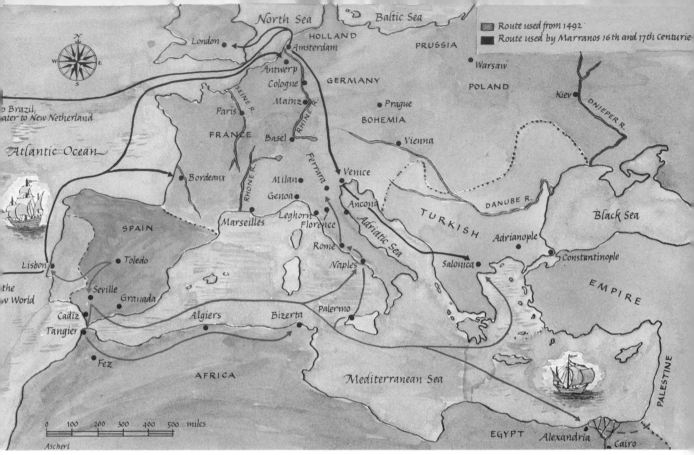

9 THE SPREAD OF SEPHARDI JEWRY

Through much of history, women served their fathers as they grew up, were sold to their husbands for payment, and served their husbands for the rest of their lives. Jewish women were generally treated with greater kindness and respect. The Talmud taught that women were not as socially important as men, but it also taught that women had full rights. Contracts of marriage, always favoring the woman, protected these rights. And the Jewish woman's role of educating children was considered holy and sacred. From time to time, women rose to leadership in Jewish communities; some, like Rashi's daughters, became great scholars.

In the sixteenth century, one Jewish woman became so important through her good works that she was called simply *La Senora,* "*The* Lady." Her full name was Dona Gracia Mendes Nasi and she lived from about 1510 to 1569.

La Senora Both before and after the edict of expulsion in 1492, Jews left Spain to escape the Inquisition and its horrors. At first, the safest nearby country was Portugal; and it was to Portugal that the family of Gracia Nasi fled. Gracia was her Jewish name, but outside the house, where she pretended to be Christian, she was called Beatrice de Luna. Even in her teens, Beatrice was beautiful, and by the time she was eighteen, she married. Her husband was Francisco Mendes, a Marrano diamond merchant and banker. Nine years later, Francisco died, leaving Beatrice a wealthy young woman.

The Angel of the Marranos Before, people had seen only her beauty, but now her wisdom shone. When the Inquisition came to Portugal, Beatrice moved her family to the Netherlands, to the city of Antwerp, and she began to use her fortune to help other Marranos escape Portugal. In 1545, she left Flanders and moved to Venice, Italy.

All this time she had remained a Marrano, still pretending outwardly to be Beatrice, the Christian. But in Venice, the government discovered that she was Jewish. They threw her into prison, and there she waited for two years while her nephew Joseph Nasi tried to ransom her. Finally, a ransom sum was agreed upon, and she was set free. There was no longer any reason to pretend, so Beatrice began using her Jewish name: Gracia Mendes Nasi.

Gracia Mendes Nasi, "Angel of the Marranos."

She and Joseph moved to Ferrara, Italy; and again she sent money to help Portuguese Jews. But even Ferrara seemed unsafe to her, and she looked elsewhere. To the east lay the Ottoman Empire of the Muslim Turks. Surely this was a place the Inquisition could not enter. But would the Turks allow the Jews to enter?

As a test, Dona Gracia herself moved to Constantinople. Here she found peace. She continued to send money to the Marranos of Portugal and to those in Italy, bringing many to live among the Turks. In her lifetime she helped so many of her people that they gave her the title, "Angel of the Marranos." So many Marranos came to settle in the Turkish empire east that a Jewish language was spoken there, a mixture of Spanish and Hebrew called *Ladino*.

Joseph Nasi   Dona Gracia's nephew, Joseph, became a loyal advisor to the sultan. In return, the sultan made him duke of the island of Naxos, and allowed him to rule many other places, including the city of Tiberias in the Holy Land. Joseph fell in love with Tiberias and ordered it rebuilt. He brought mulberry trees and silkworms from the Far East to start a silk industry there. Then he sent an invitation to the Jews of Italy. Legend tells that one shipload of Italian Jews arrived in the Holy Land only to be captured by pirates and sold into slavery. Few others dared to come. For Joseph it was a great disappointment. Yet his years at the court of the sultan were good years for the Jews of the Ottoman Empire.

The Reformation and the Jews of Holland   Not all Sephardi Jews headed to Turkey. Just as Gracia Nasi had done at first, many went to the Low Countries, especially Holland. It was the time of the Reformation in Europe, when the Catholic church split in two. The new movement was called Protestant because it "protested" the Catholic way of life. The people of Holland, the Dutch, were among the new Protestants. They revolted against Catholic Spain; and in 1579 became an independent country.

Among the Dutch, the Jews found new freedoms. By 1598, the Jews of Amsterdam were allowed to build a synagogue and to practice Judaism openly. From Holland, the Jews spread westward, too. A Dutch Jew, Manasseh ben Israel, traveled to England to meet the Protestant leader, Oliver Cromwell. The Jews had been expelled from England in 1290, but Manasseh convinced Cromwell to allow them to return. Thus the Jews of Spain scattered to new parts of the world and returned to places where Jews had not been seen for many generations.

Jews of Holland, as painted by the great master artist, Rembrandt.

BARUCH SPINOZA

Baruch Spinoza was born in Amsterdam, Holland in 1632. His parents came from Portugal, fleeing the Inquisition. Spinoza studied Talmud and Bible, but also philosophy; and he created a new way of thinking, a philosophy built on logic and mathematics. In his writings, he argued against many Jewish and Christian teachings. His idea that God was a part of the natural world seemed both strange and dangerous to the Jews of Amsterdam.

Because they could not accept this idea, and because they were afraid the Christians would blame the spread of Spinoza's teachings on the Jewish community, the Jews finally excommunicated Spinoza. To be excommunicated by the rabbis meant being cut off from the Jewish community forever. It was the harshest punishment for a Jew; and it made Baruch Spinoza into a person without a people.

Reading his works today, we can see that many of Spinoza's ideas are like those of many modern thinkers. To us they do not seem either strange or difficult. In his own time, the Jews of Holland judged against him; but the way of thinking he created was not lost: it became the starting point for all modern thought.

Baruch Spinoza

A TIME OF CHANGE

By the seventeenth century, the Jews of Ashkenaz and the Jews of Sepharad shared many things in common. Both lived deeply Jewish lives. Both had a history of suffering and persecution, and an equally long history of faith and study. Both had given rise to wonderful communities, with long traditions of charity and good works.

Now the most important Sephardi communities were in places like Amsterdam, Holland; Turkey; North Africa; and the New World—North and South America. And the most important Ashkenazi communities were in Germany and Poland.

Great changes were about to take place, mainly among the Jews of the north. These changes would occur because the church would soon be split into Catholics and Protestants, because new governments in many places would break free of the church entirely, and because Christian thinkers would begin to take the idea of freedom seriously. Soon the ghetto walls would fall. Even the shtetls would learn of new freedoms and new ideas coming from the west. Soon industry and science would change the way people everywhere thought—about themselves, about the world. Hard times were not over for the Jews. Persecution and suffering would continue to plague them; but now a small light began to shine in the distance, and Jewish hopes were set aflame.

10 MADMAN, MESSIAH, AND MASTER

The Madman   In 1648, Bogdan Chmielnicki raised an army of Cossack horsemen and led them in a revolution against the rulers of Poland. The Jews were caught in the middle. Since the Jews were often agents of the Poles, collecting taxes and managing farms and forests, Chmielnicki swore to destroy every Jew living in the area called the Ukraine—and he almost succeeded.

For two bloody years, the Cossacks attacked. More than 300 towns were destroyed; more than 100,000 Jews were slaughtered. Thousands of Jews were forced to convert. Those who refused were cruelly tortured, whipped to death, or drowned in the rivers of Poland. Holy books were thrown into the streets. The scrolls of the Torah were cut into sandals for the Cossacks to wear. Thousands of Jews were homeless, wandering through the countryside in search of a place of safety.

This was a deep shock to the Jews of Poland. One rabbi wrote that these massacres were a "Third Destruction . . . which was the same as the First and Second Destructions [of the ancient Temples]."

Chmielnicki's rebellion against Poland succeeded, and the land of the Cossacks became a part of Russia. Despite the horror of the murdering and the pillaging, the Polish Jews slowly rebuilt their homes, their towns and villages.

False Messiahs   Many times in Jewish history, the Jews believed that the days of the Messiah were close at hand. In the terrible days of the Inquisition, in 1524, a Jew named David Reuveni claimed that he had been sent to Venice, Italy by the Ten Lost Tribes of Israel (the tribes enslaved by the Assyrians when the ancient Kingdom of Israel was destroyed). Reuveni said that he had come to form a union between Christians and Jews to drive the Turks from the Holy Land. For a time he was taken seriously. He was even allowed to speak with the Pope. And the Jews, seeing this, believed that the Messiah had truly come to save them.

As terrifying as a blazing forest fire, the Cossacks rode through the Jewish villages destroying all in their path.

But, in the end, Reuveni was arrested. He was thrown into prison and later was burned at the stake by the Inquisition. His chief follower, Solomon Molcho, who had been a Portuguese Marrano, was also burned at the stake by the Inquisition. The story of Reuveni is just one of many in the history of false Messiahs who would raise the hopes of the Jews only to disappoint them. By far the strangest story is that of a Turkish Jew, Shabbetai Zevi.

The Man Who Called Himself Messiah

In 1654, shortly after the Cossack massacres that had been called the "Third Destruction," Shabbetai Zevi announced that he was the Messiah. His teachings, (based in part on the teachings of Isaac Luria) were simple enough for the majority of Jews to accept; and his followers truly believed that Shabbetai had come to lead the people of Israel to the Holy Land. Not only the Jews and Marranos in Turkey, where he lived, were caught up in this Messiah-fever, but also Jews from Poland and the rest of Europe.

Jewish merchants closed their shops and packed their belongings. In ragtag caravans they marched toward Turkey to join Shabbetai Zevi. They were bound for Palestine, hoping the days of the Messiah had come.

In 1666, Shabbetai was taken prisoner in Adrianople, Turkey by the sultan. The Turkish government was alarmed by all this Jewish fervor. They offered Shabbetai a simple choice: either convert to Islam or be killed on the spot. Shabbetai converted.

An anti-Jewish riot in 16th century Germany.

Word of the conversion spread among the Jews waiting at the Turkish border. Many simply refused to believe it. Some said that Shabbetai had only pretended to convert, waiting for the right time to declare his Jewishness again. The right time never came. Shabbetai Zevi died a Muslim. The disappointment was heavy. Large numbers of Jews had lost everything. They were broken in spirit, penniless, and homeless.

The Split in Jewish Life

The Jews slowly became aware that a serious division was opening up between the average Jew and the scholars. Great schools of

Rabbis in Tzfat still study in the same way as their fathers did.

learning, yeshivahs, had always existed but in the new yeshivahs the study of Torah and Talmud became more and more removed from real life. Much of it was *pilpul* (from the Hebrew word for "pepper"), based on little points of law that had no real importance for the vast majority of Jews.

While these schools were famous in Poland and Lithuania, the governments there began to demand new and heavier taxes of the Jews. Most Jews worked from sunup to sundown just to purchase food for their families. Many had no time at all to study Torah; and they felt guilty because they did not know how to follow God's laws properly. Not only were they poor, but they felt that only great scholars could live a true Jewish life.

The Master Then, about 250 years ago, news passed from village to village of a new movement called *Hasidism*, "Piousness." Its leader was Israel ben Eliezer, called the *Ba'al Shem Tov* ("Master of [God's] Good Name), or just the *Besht* (from the initial letters of *Ba'al Shem Tov*). The Besht taught that any Jew could live a good and full Jewish life—even without being a great Jewish scholar! It was important for a Jew to cling to God as the Torah and prayer book said, "with all your heart, with all your soul, and with all your might." This "clinging" or *devekut* (which Luria had called kavvanah) could be found while praying, observing one of the commandments, or even while drinking, singing, dancing, or eating. The Besht taught that a Jew's whole life should be filled with joy and gladness. Any Jew could be a mystic; learned or simple, rich or poor.

In fact, he taught, it was easier for a poor person to cling to God than for a rich person. The rich one had to stop thinking of money and possessions, but the poor person had God as riches!

For the simple, hard-working Jews, Hasidism breathed new life into Judaism. It was easy to understand; it was enjoyable to practice. And the stories and fables told by the *maggidim*, the Hasidic "storytellers," and the teachings of the holy *tsaddikim* ("righteous ones"), as many Hasidic leaders were called, delighted the people and filled their hearts with a new love for Judaism.

Jews in the time of the Ba'al Shem Tov.

Tzfat today.

TZFAT, CITY OF MYSTICS

Throughout history some Jews have always lived in the Land of Israel. And, at times, there have even been large movements of Jews from the Diaspora back to the Holy Land. In fact, in the 1500s, the city of Tzfat (Safed) had become an important Jewish community. The great teacher, Joseph Caro (see chapter five) was the head of a famous academy there; and Tzfat had also become the center of the study of Jewish mysticism (see chapter four).

Around 1570, the most important teacher of mysticism and of the Zohar was Isaac Luria of Tzfat. He died after teaching only two years, but it took his students ten

THE MITNAGGEDIM

The Hasidic movement troubled the scholars in their academies. Scholars felt that this new kind of Judaism would lead Jews away from the study of Torah and Talmud. They did not mind the rejoicing, but they objected to the superstitions that Hasidim taught to their followers. It was claimed that Hasidic rebbes could work "miracles," and that the amulets or charms they made for their followers could protect people from evil and disaster. All this seemed very un-Jewish. To combat Hasidism, a new movement appeared called *Mitnaggedut*, the "Opposition" to the Hasidic movement.

The greatest of the *Mitnaggedim* was Rabbi Elijah of

years to record all they had learned. Lovingly, they remembered Luria as *Ha-Ari*, "The Lion."

From Tzfat, Luria's teachings spread throughout the Jewish world. He taught that in the beginning, when God created the universe, God's light was too strong for the vessels that were supposed to hold it. The vessels broke, mixing light and darkness, good and evil. Through concentration and devotion (kavannah), human beings can help the sparks of light rise upward again. This work is called *tikkun*, "repair"; and it is the holy work assigned to all who wish to bring the days of the Messiah closer.

Vilna, whose learning in Talmud was so deep that he was known as the *Vilna Gaon* ("The Genius of Vilna"). Oddly enough, the Vilna Gaon was known for another kind of Jewish learning, too: the study of Kabbalah—Jewish mysticism.

Thus, as the modern age began, the largest community of Jews in Europe was split into two camps—Hasidim and Mitnaggedim. Each camp believed that its way was the proper way of Torah. Rabbis in the two groups even began to excommunicate (ban from Jewish life) one another. It seemed that the world of Judaism was about to split in two. Yet a common bond held the two movements closely together: the love of Torah.

11 HASKALAH: THE ENLIGHTENMENT

Court Jews In the mid-1700s, Germany was divided into many small states. The largest was Prussia, ruled by Frederick the Great. Under Frederick's leadership, Prussia became a homeland for many of the finest writers of Europe. Voltaire, the French thinker, lived at Frederick's court for a while. Goethe and Lessing, two of the finest minds of the time, made Prussia their home. And Prussia became one of the main centers for a new movement called the Enlightenment.

The Jews of Prussia, like most German Jews, still lived in ghettos. By day, they left the ghettos to do business as peddlers and moneylenders—there were few other jobs for them. By night, the ghetto gates were locked and guarded. To the Jews and the Christians alike, this seemed a natural way of life.

But Frederick, and many of the rulers of the small German states who tried to imitate him, thought that "special" Jews should be given "special" rights and privileges. So a few Jews—sometimes the brightest, sometimes the richest—were allowed to live outside the ghettos in cities like Berlin. They were called Court Jews, since their rights came from the courts of the princes and kings.

In return for these special rights, the Court Jews loaned money to the kings and princes, watched over the minting of silver coins to be used in trade, and helped to establish factories and railroads. Because they trusted one another, Court Jews in different states were able to set up international banking and trade. Living side by side with Christians, they often dressed like non-Jews and spoke French and German. Often the Court Jews were made the heads of the Jewish communities as well.

A Court Jew who became the spokesperson for a Jewish community was called a *shtadlan* or "pleader." A shtadlan could sometimes arrange for other Jews to move outside the ghettos, or for bright Jewish youngsters to study at Christian universities. Slowly, in cities like Frankfort, Hamburg, and Berlin, small Jewish communities grew up of Jews with special rights. One who was given special permission to live in Berlin was Moses Mendelssohn.

Mendelssohn, "Father of the Haskalah"

Mendelssohn was born in Dessau, Germany, in 1729. There he studied Talmud, and became a favorite pupil of his rabbi. When the rabbi moved to Berlin in 1743, Moses Mendelssohn followed him. In Berlin, he continued his Jewish studies, but added to them the study of Latin, English, French, and Ital-

While Jews had been shut into ghettos, the cities of Europe grew more and more beautiful. Such was the scene that greeted the eyes of the first Court Jews in Dresden.

ian; and also subjects such as history, mathematics, logic, and philosophy.

Though he always remained an Orthodox Jew, Mendelssohn's imagination was captured by the world of modern ideas. He wrote a short book of philosophy that made him famous throughout Europe, and he was admired by many of the great Christian scholars of his time. He discovered among these thinkers a new and revolutionary idea, the idea that every person has certain basic rights just because that person is born human. This idea would soon change the shape of the world. In America, it would lead to the American Revolution and the Constitution with its Bill of Rights for all citizens. In France, it would lead to the French Revolution with its battle cry of "liberty, equality, and fraternity (brotherhood)."

Mendelssohn was thrilled by the thought that Jews would soon be equal to their Christian neighbors, and would soon be freed from the ghettos and the years of living apart. But were the Jews ready for this freedom? They still lived the life of the Middle Ages, while around them a new age was dawning, the Age of Reason. They spoke Yiddish, the language of Ashkenazi Jews since the Middle Ages. They could not even read the books filled with the new ideas that excited him.

To help the Jews, Mendelssohn and his students and followers decided to teach them to read German. They translated the Torah into the German language. This translation was printed in Hebrew characters alongside the Hebrew of the Torah. Now the Jews could study German through the study of Torah. And many did. Then they used the German language to read other books, among them the books of Mendelssohn himself. Through Mendelssohn's work, the Jews began to learn the ideas of the modern world. This they called *Haskalah* or "Enlightenment"; and they called Mendelssohn the "father of Haskalah."

Mendelssohn had hoped that teaching his people modern ideas would prepare them for freedom. But it did not. Freedom came like a bolt of lightning that tears a limb from a tree. In the confusion about what freedom meant, many Jews were lost to Judaism forever. As the ten lost tribes of ancient times had faded among the Assyrians, so many modern Jews faded into the German states and the French state and the American nations. The questions that troubled Mendelssohn and his followers are the same questions that we must answer every day—the questions of making the right choices, of using freedom in the right ways.

NEW CHRISTIAN PRESSURES

Through most of Western Europe, the church no longer forced Jews to convert. But now it was hinted that conversion would make life easier for the Jew who wanted more freedom. It was that kind of hint that first upset Moses Mendelssohn. A Christian minister said that Mendelssohn was a true philosopher. Therefore, the minister argued, Mendelssohn should become a Christian, since Christianity was the true religion of the philosophers.

Mendelssohn had hardly written about Judaism up to this time. He thought religion was a private, not a public matter. But now he felt forced to defend it. Comparing Judaism and Christianity to a two-story house in which Judaism was the base or first story, Mendelssohn wrote:

Moses Mendelssohn

If it were true that the cornerstones of my house are so out of line that the entire building seems about to collapse, would I act wisely if I tried to save my belongings simply by moving them from the lower to the upper floor? Would I be safer there? Christianity, as you know, is built upon Judaism and would therefore collapse along with it.

12 THE EMAN- CIPATION

Napoleon and the Jews The French Revolution came in 1789, bringing the new freedom of which the thinkers of the Enlightenment had dreamed. The word *citizen* took on new meaning. It meant a person was equal in every way to all the other persons in a nation. Farmers were citizens, and so were princes and kings and nobles. People greeted one another on the streets with the words, "Hello, citizen."

Two years passed before the citizens of France decided that the Jews should also be citizens. For the Jews of France, emancipation came in 1791. And even though they had been made to wait, it was a great moment in the history of our people in Europe. It was the first time since the days of the Romans that Jews were made equal under the law of the people amongst whom they lived.

Napoleon hoped to make the Jews loyal subjects of France. To this end, he called 111 famous and noted Jewish authorities together in 1807, calling this the Grand Sanhedrin.

And now, as the nineteenth century began, the armies of France, led by the brilliant general Napoleon Bonaparte, conquered much of Europe. Wherever his armies were victorious, Napoleon freed the Jews. When he was defeated, many countries tried to restore the old order, but they could not turn back the clock. The world had entered the Age of Reason, and the Jews would be a part of it. For the Jews, emancipation once begun did not end.

Even the Jews of Eastern Europe heard the bells of liberty ringing. They moved to larger cities, or they began to discuss the emancipation in the marketplaces of their shtetls.

Judaism and Christianity   Once free, the Jews were allowed to enter universities and to study side by side with Christians. Physics and history, chemistry and philosophy, art and poetry—all doors seemed to open at once. Things were not perfect, of course. Many Christians still would not allow Jews to enter their homes. Sometimes Jews were not allowed to graduate from the university unless they were willing to convert. Jews still could not own land; many professions were still closed to them. And the hundreds of years of anti-Jewish teaching, the terrible work of prejudice that the church had accomplished—that did not die easily and, in some ways, did not die at all.

Pride in Being Jewish   While they were in the ghetto, the Jews believed that their way of life was better than the life outside the ghetto. Jews lived by laws of kindness and justice, at a time when Christians cruelly tortured one another and ruled over one another by force.

But now to Jews leaving the ghetto, the world seemed changed. Perhaps because they were locked in the ghetto so long they had not noticed the changes before. Napoleon's laws seemed fair and just. The churches, Protestant and Catholic, taught people to read and write; and the new states did so, too. There was more talk in the world about charity and kindness, even if it was not always easy to find it. And— truly the most amazing thing of all—the Jews were being welcomed to join this new society as equals.

THE MOST FAMOUS CONVERT

A close friend of Zunz, and one of the members of the Society for the Culture and Science of Judaism, was the German Jewish poet, Heinrich Heine. Heine was twenty-five years old when his first book of poetry made him famous, and he joined the Society in that same year. But to get his degree from the university at Göttingen, Heine had to convert to Christianity. Now the Jews thought of him as an outsider; and Heine was trapped between two worlds, the Jewish and the Christian, belonging to neither.

His conversion troubled him greatly. In 1850 he said, "I make no secret of my Judaism, to which I have never returned, because I never left it." He studied the Bible and called it a "treasure," saying that the Jews of the Middle Ages had carried it with them as if it were a "portable homeland." Even as he lay dying, he called himself a "poor, deathly sick Jew."

Surely many of the assimilated and converted Jews were like Heine, learning how much of a treasure they had lost only after they had lost it.

Heinrich Heine

Some Jews looked at the way of life of the ghetto and saw that it had not changed since the twelfth century. It looked old and ragged somehow, like a worn-out piece of clothing. They turned away from it, they *assimilated*—they stopped practicing the laws of Judaism and following the Jewish way of life. They tried to become "normal" Germans or French or Britishers. They did not convert to Christianity, they just tried to forget they were Jewish.

Some converted. No one was forcing them to convert, but converting made it easier to get ahead in the world outside the ghetto. Surprisingly, converting was not always good for these Jews. The Christians never forgot who was originally Jewish and who was not. They looked down upon the converts, and often would not befriend them. Many an ex-Jew found that conversion was a terrible trap.

The Science of Judaism   Other Jews set out to make Judaism more modern. Among them was Leopold Zunz. He started a group called the Society for the Culture and Science of Judaism. Zunz and his Society studied the ancient texts of Judaism using the new scientific methods of the nineteenth century. They hoped to teach assimilated Jews to be proud of their Jewish tradition, not embarrassed by it. Their studies were brilliant; Zunz was a genius. But the assimilated Jews of Berlin paid hardly any attention at all, and in a short time the Society collapsed.

Nevertheless, Zunz continued his work. To the Jews who believed that the Jewish way of life had never changed, Zunz proved that it had always been changing and growing, that it had always met new problems with new answers. He was sure that there were new answers for the problem of being modern, too, answers that would give the Jews new pride in their Jewishness. In the ways he studied, Zunz was modern. In his deep faith and belief in Judaism, he was like the great Jewish thinkers and teachers of the Middle Ages.

UNIT FOUR

THE WAY WE LIVE TODAY

In the nineteenth century, the tree of Jewish life branched out in new directions. Two great movements, Reform and Conservative Judaism, began and grew. Traditional Jews formed a third, Orthodox, movement. The Science of Judaism blossomed and was turned to the study of Torah, history, and customs as you are studying them now. Zionism, a movement calling for a national home for the Jews, became an important part of Jewish life.

As the number of Jewish choices became richer, each Jew faced the question we still ask today: What does *being Jewish* mean? To answer it, our story must become three stories. One tells how the Jews came to the shores of North America and built here a great center of Jewish life. Another tells what became of the Jews of Europe and how the Holocaust happened. And the third tells how our people returned at last to its Promised Land, how they built the State of Israel.

13 THE FIRST JEWS IN NORTH AMERICA

The first Jews in North America settled in New Amsterdam, a Dutch colony on the Hudson River, in 1654. They were poor, and had suffered much. The Portuguese drove them from their South American home in Recife, Brazil. As they sailed northward, their ship was attacked and captured by pirates who planned to sell them into slavery. A storm came up that wrecked the pirate ship and the Jews were stranded for a time on an island. They were rescued by a French captain who took what little money they had left, and in return for this payment set them ashore in New Amsterdam.

Peter Stuyvesant greeted them with suspicion. Stuyvesant was the governor of New Amsterdam, appointed by the Dutch West Indies Company of Holland. He was a strict man, more a soldier than a governor; and when he saw the Jews were penniless, he allowed them to stay only if they promised never to take charity from the Christians. To the Jews, taking care of their own poor and needy had always been a part of keeping their ancient Covenant. They gladly agreed to Stuyvesant's condition.

Still, Stuyvesant did not trust them. Once he refused to allow the Jews to stand guard along the city wall, a duty that all citizens of New Amsterdam shared. But the Jews wrote directly to the Dutch West Indies Company, and the company ordered Stuyvesant to grant Jews this right. The Jews stood guard proudly; they won their first small fight for equal rights.

In time, the British took over New Amsterdam and renamed it New York. It became through the years a center of Jewish life and culture, so that one modern writer called it, "the greatest Jewish city in the world."

Jews in Other Colonies   Jews from the Sephardi countries continued to settle in North America in the seventeenth century, in places like Georgia, Pennsylvania, South Carolina, and Quebec. For the most part, they

The old Mill St. Synagogue in New York City.

The interior of the Touro Synagogue, oldest standing synagogue in the United States. Though the congregation was Ashkenazi, the building and the service were "in the American manner," Sephardi. (Below) A plaque set up in 1947 declares the synagogue a National Historical Site.

arrived in small groups. The first action they took as a community was to purchase land for a Jewish cemetery, for they lived according to the Jewish laws they had followed in Europe and North Africa. When they built synagogues, they prayed according to Sephardi rituals and sang the melodies of Spain and Portugal; and their synagogues became the center of their lives.

In 1658, a small community of Ashkenazi Jews came from northern Europe and settled among the Protestants of Rhode Island. This colony had been founded by a young Protestant minister, Roger Williams, who believed that people of all religions should be treated equally. He soon gave the Jews full rights, allowing them to build a synagogue. Strange to say, when their sanctuary was complete, the Ashkenazi Jews of Rhode Island chose to pray according to the Sephardi customs.

Jews in the colonies were soapmakers, tobacconists, saddlers, bakers, tailors, merchants, and silversmiths—and in Canada, fur traders. In addition to maintaining the cemetery and the synagogue, they lived closely together in order to observe the laws of kashrut, and community funds were directed toward charity for the poor and for newcomers. Synagogues often had a cantor, and sometimes a preacher, but there were no rabbis in America until 1840.

Sharing   Unlike the Jews in Europe, American Jews shared the life of their non-Jewish neighbors. They lived and worked side by side with other immigrants, struggling to erect new cities and to improve the life in those already established. By the time of the American Revolution, there were strong Jewish communities in New York, New-

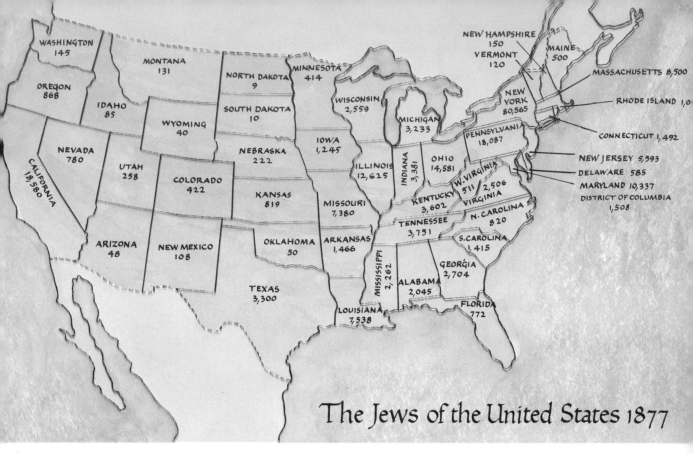

The Jews of the United States 1877

Map showing Jewish population by state: WASHINGTON 145, OREGON 868, IDAHO 85, MONTANA 131, NORTH DAKOTA 9, SOUTH DAKOTA 10, MINNESOTA 414, WISCONSIN 2,559, WYOMING 40, NEBRASKA 222, IOWA 1,245, MICHIGAN 3,233, NEVADA 780, UTAH 258, COLORADO 422, KANSAS 819, MISSOURI 7,380, ILLINOIS 12,625, INDIANA 3,381, OHIO 14,581, CALIFORNIA 18,580, ARIZONA 48, NEW MEXICO 108, OKLAHOMA 50, ARKANSAS 1,466, TENNESSEE 3,751, KENTUCKY 3,602, W. VIRGINIA 511, VIRGINIA 2,506, N. CAROLINA 820, TEXAS 3,300, LOUISIANA 7,538, MISSISSIPPI 2,262, ALABAMA 2,045, GEORGIA 2,704, S. CAROLINA 1,415, FLORIDA 772, NEW HAMPSHIRE 150, VERMONT 120, MAINE 500, MASSACHUSETTS 8,500, RHODE ISLAND 1,0, NEW YORK 80,565, CONNECTICUT 1,492, PENNSYLVANIA 18,087, NEW JERSEY 5,593, DELAWARE 585, MARYLAND 10,337, DISTRICT OF COLUMBIA 1,508

port, Charlestown (now Charleston), Savannah, Montreal, and Philadelphia.

The Philadelphia synagogue was built with some money given by non-Jews such as Benjamin Franklin. Asser Levy of New York gave money to the Lutherans to help them build their first New York church. In this way, Jews and Gentiles helped one another in religious life even as they helped one another in business matters.

Jews and the Revolution   By the time of the American Revolution, there were about 2,500 Jews living in North America. Some remained loyal to Great Britain, but many more had come to believe in the kind of freedom demanded by the Declaration of Independence of 1776, that "All men are created equal . . . they are endowed by their Creator with certain unalienable Rights, that among these are Life, Liberty, and the pursuit of Happiness."

A wealthy Newport merchant, Aaron Lopez, lost almost his entire fortune—not only money, but even his fleet of 113 ships—helping America to win the revolutionary war. The first Polish Jew mentioned in American history, Haym Salomon, also lost his fortune by making loans and donations to the young government of the Revolution, and especially to the ragged and poor army of General George Washington.

It was not by chance that when the Founding Fathers of the United States ordered a special bell to be cast to ring out the new message of freedom, the Liberty Bell, they chose a verse from the Torah to be inscribed on it: "Proclaim Liberty throughout the land unto all the inhabitants thereof."

AMERICAN VALUES, JEWISH VALUES

The Puritans' way of life, based on hard work and "high moral behavior" (acting rightly), became the backbone of our American way of life. Since these rules had been learned from the Bible, the Puritans were really bringing Jewish ideals to America. Part of their heritage is the harvest festival of Thanksgiving which is based on the Jewish harvest festival of Sukkot. Both come at about the same time of the year; and both give thanks to God for providing food from the earth.

Ideas of democracy were also learned from the Bible. These were the values of freedom and equality, of religious tolerance and liberty. In Europe, Mendelssohn and his followers were writing about these ideas. In America, Jews were already living by them day by day. When the new State of Virginia passed its law "Establishing Religious Freedom" in 1785, it was the first law in history to grant full rights to all persons whatever their religion. And when the Constitution of the United States was adopted in 1789, Jews were given every right of citizenship, even the right to run for public office. To the Jews escaping the terrors of the Inquisition or the hardships of the ghetto, the United States was the answer to a dream.

14 GERMAN JEWS COME TO AMERICA

Separation of Church and State In Europe, the church had been a part of the government. In America, Thomas Jefferson, John Madison, and others argued that the church should be apart from the government so that each person would be free to practice any religion. When the United States government was set up and the Bill of Rights written, the "wall of separation" between church and state was made law. Slowly, each of the states—even those founded by church leaders—accepted this idea and guaranteed freedom of religion. The Jews of America found themselves free to be both citizens and Jews.

Jewish Leaders and Citizens How did they use this new freedom? The answer is, in many ways.

Judah Touro (his father helped build the Newport synagogue now called the Touro Synagogue) moved to New Orleans. There he fought with General Andrew Jackson against the British in the War of 1812. After the war, he became a merchant, donated money to building churches and synagogues (there is a Touro Synagogue in New Orleans named after him), helped the poor, and built up the trade of the port of New Orleans. He was a leader in the Jewish community and the New Orleans community as well.

Mordecai Manuel Noah was a writer of plays, a leader of New York society, a sheriff of New York county, a judge, and served for a time as the United States Consul to Tunis. While he was in Tunis, Noah saw the poor Jews of North Africa and took pity on them. He bought an island in the Niagara River near Buffalo, New York, and sent out a proclamation calling for the Jewish people "to be gathered from the four corners of

Many Jews left the port cities and ventured into the frontiers, trading with farmers and backwoods settlers, as the Yankee peddlers had traded in New England a generation before.

the globe. . . ." Few Jews came. Noah's grand plan for creating a Jewish state in North America failed. But he began to believe that Palestine was the true answer for the poor Jews of the world; and, in this way, he became an early Zionist.

Uriah P. Levy spent much of his life fighting against prejudice in the armed services. Jews had been serving in the military since the time of George Washington, but many military people were anti-Jewish or felt that Jews did not make good soldiers. Levy joined the United States Navy and in every way became a fine officer, proving by his actions that Jews could be brave and loyal. He had to fight for his rights at every turn, but in the end he became the first Jew to reach the Navy's highest rank, Commodore.

American Jews saw people like Touro, Noah, and Levy as models. Jews could take pride in what these people achieved, both for their people and for their country.

The German Immigration   Beginning around 1825, a great wave of immigrants came from the countries of northern Europe to the United States — and among them were many Ashkenazi Jews. In 1850 there were only about 45,000 Jews in America; 30 years later, there were almost 400,000! Many were able to come because the ocean voyage had become more common. Ships now regularly crossed the Atlantic Ocean; passage could be bought with little money. Of course, the Ashkenazi Jews were not often rich. But in cities like Prague, Berlin, and Vienna, there were Jewish Immigration Societies that helped by giving them loans. Buying the cheapest tickets, the Jews traveled in "steerage," that is, herded together in close quarters, sleeping on wooden shelves in the bellies of the ships. They thought only of America, suffering willingly the few weeks it took to make the journey.

Many left their families behind, intending to bring them later. Brother sent for brother, sister sent for sister; children sent for their parents and husbands for their wives and children, until whole families had been transplanted. They hoped to share in the riches of the new world; and to escape the oppression and poverty of the old world.

JEWS ON THE FRONTIER

The Jews settled mainly in the large cities of the East Coast, but some set out to follow the trails westward, becoming pioneers in a time of pioneering. The Jewish "pioneers" were peddlers carrying needles and thread, pots and pans, rags and combs, scissors and cloth in bags slung across their shoulders. Often they walked long distances from farm to farm selling their goods. And everywhere they went they were welcome since they brought not only merchandise, but news of neighbors and of the world, too.

Saving their money, many bought wagons or buggies and bigger stocks of goods to sell. If they found a place they liked, they would settle down and open a general store or a dry goods (clothing) business. Soon there were Jews in Cincinnati, Chicago, Milwaukee, and many other Midwestern towns. And still other Jews followed the trails to cities like Denver, Dallas, and San Francisco.

In 1849, the Jews of San Francisco set up a tent and held a Yom Kippur service. And around that time, one Jewish peddler named Levi Strauss began to make heavy trousers called "Levis" to sell to miners and prospectors during the years of the gold rush.

The "Indian Wigwam" store in the old west.

Years of War

In 1861 the Jews of America found themselves divided by the Civil War, "The War Between the States." Judah P. Benjamin, a Jewish plantation owner, became secretary of war (later secretary of state) for the Confederate (southern) government. Rabbi Isaac Mayer Wise of Cincinnati spoke out for the South, while his friend Rabbi David Einhorn of Baltimore was forced to leave Maryland because he spoke out against the South and against slavery.

After the war was over in 1865, the Jews turned again to the task of earning their way. Clearly, these Jews were very different from their parents who had lived in ghettos. In almost every way they were a part of the life of the new nation, a part of its politics and of its troubles—and a part of its glories. In America, they were equals in a land of equals.

Years of Fortune

The 1800s were years of building. Some Jews went from "rags to riches" in their own lifetimes. The Straus brothers joined a small New York company called R.H. Macy and turned it into the world's largest department store. Other Jewish names such as Gimbel and Altman also became famous through department store fortunes. Some Jews earned wealth in banking—the Seligmans and Warburgs, among these. And there were Jewish writers, painters, and thinkers. Freedom did not always lead to great wealth; and most Jews did not grow rich. Most worked hard, saved their money, and improved their lives little by little.

Times were good—very good, indeed. Jews continued to observe the traditions of their people, especially through charity. They founded societies to help the poor, hospitals where Jewish doctors practiced and kosher food was available, Hebrew literary societies—these later became the

The employees of S. Lazarus, Sons & Co. proudly pose for a group portrait outside their store.

"Abraham and Strauss" started out in a wagon.

Young Men's Hebrew Association—social clubs such as the Independent Order of B'nai B'rith, orphanages for Jewish and non-Jewish children, and other charitable organizations. They helped bring more Jews from Europe and helped new immigrants to settle and find work. Thus they honored the Covenant of ancient times, while also honoring their covenant with America—to take care of their own.

They aided in the building of public libraries and town halls, monuments and civic centers. They continued to build synagogues wherever they went and to purchase land for Jewish cemeteries. Tzedakah and the synagogue were together the core of American Jewish life.

REASONS FOR COMING TO AMERICA
What made so many Jews from Europe come to the United States in the 1850s?

For one thing, new industries in Europe were bringing people from the farms to the cities. Cities grew large and overcrowded. Often there was not enough work to go around; and what work there was, was given first to Christians. Jewish workers found it hard to get jobs in Europe. So, many turned to America where work was plentiful.

For some there was another reason, too. In 1830 and 1848, many European countries were rocked by revolutions. These wars against royalty were fought by those who believed in the ideals of the Age of Reason, ideals of freedom and equality. But the revolutions ended in failure. The revolutionaries were forced to flee for their lives; and Christians and Jews alike, they made their way to the shores of America.

15 JEWISH LIFE IN EUROPE

Freedom Officially, the Jews became citizens of France in 1791. Years later, other European countries began to accept Jews as full citizens: Belgium, in 1830; Denmark, in 1849; Austria, in 1867; Germany, in 1869; Italy, in 1870; Sweden and Switzerland, late in the 1870s; and Norway, much later, in 1891. In all, it took nearly one hundred years for the Jews to gain full rights of citizenship in Western Europe. The laws of the Middle Ages which had kept the Jews in ghettos were disappearing. But some of the old anti-Jewish feelings did not pass away so easily.

For centuries, as you read in Unit One, hatred of the Jews had arisen out of superstition and the preachings of the

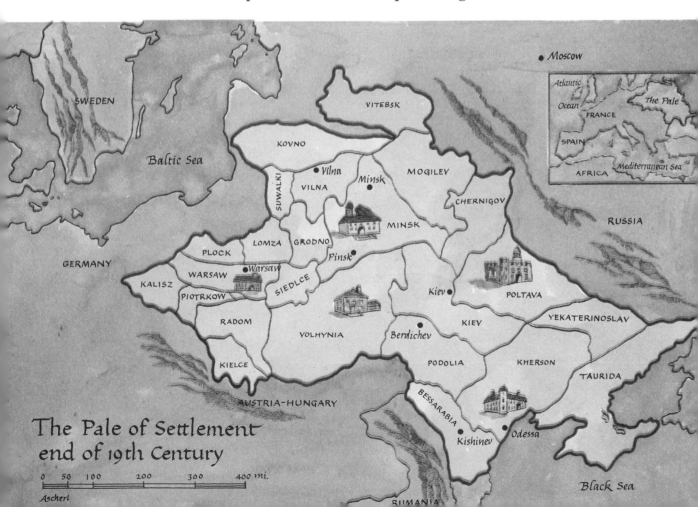

The Pale of Settlement
end of 19th Century

0   50   100   200   300   400 mi.

Ascherl

church. The church—especially local priests—taught the lie that the Jews were "Christ-killers," murderers of Jesus. In the Middle Ages, Jews had been accused of poisoning wells and causing the Black Death that swept over Europe. Often they were accused of the *blood libel*, killing Christians to use their blood in baking Passover matzah. To educated people of the 1800s, these superstitions and lies seemed ridiculous; but there were many uneducated people who continued to believe and teach them.

The Damascus Blood Libel   In 1840, a Catholic priest disappeared in the city of Damascus, Syria. In those days, Damascus was such a dangerous place that murder, robbery, and kidnapping were common. But the Syrian police were informed that the missing priest had probably been murdered by the Jews for his blood. Suddenly, all the fears and superstitions rose again. The Syrian police arrested many Jews—men, women, and even children. They tortured the Jews, forcing a few to "confess." Of course, the moment the torture ended, the Jews who had "confessed" made it clear that they had done so only to save their lives. They knew nothing of the priest or his disappearance.

Throughout the world, Jews read of the blood libel in their newspapers and were shocked. They wrote magazine articles, letters to the editors of newspapers, and letters to their governments in protest. Every Jewish leader took part in this campaign. Two families—Moses Montefiore and his wife Judith, and Adolphe Cremieux and his wife—were sent to Damascus to speak for all of world Jewry. They called on the sultan of Syria to release the Jews being held in prison and to admit that the charges against the Jews were false.

In the end it was not truth, but business and world opinion that won the day. Syria was a poor country, relying in part on Jewish banks. That, combined with pressures from many western governments, forced the governor to see the "wisdom" of reconsidering. Not only were the prisoners released and an official statement made that they were totally inno-

When the pogrom broke out in Kiev, Jews were beaten and wounded while the police looked on.

cent, but Montefiore received from the sultan a statement condemning the blood libel and affirming Jewish rights. Returning home to France, the Montefiores and the Cremieuxs were greeted as heroes by Jews and non-Jews alike. The Jews had learned a lesson, too. Despite the new freedoms, Jews would still have to fight against old prejudices.

The Jews of Russia The need of the Jews for protection was especially clear in Russia under the czars. Russia had expelled all its Jews in 1727; but in 1772, 1793, and in 1795, Russia took over parts of Poland that contained hundreds of thousands of Jews. To keep the Jews from spreading throughout her kingdom, Czarina Catherine II created the "Pale of Settlement." An imaginary line was drawn inside the old boundaries of what had been the Polish land, and the Polish Jews were forced to stay within that line. Laws were passed to encourage the Jews to leave altogether, but the Jews—most of them poor—could not raise the money to escape. In the end, the Jews were simply told they could not leave the Pale of Settlement at all.

A NEW SENSE OF UNITY

The Damascus Blood Libel, and the way in which Jews of many countries had worked together, gave the Jews of Europe a sense of unity. For the first time the idea of the *shtadlan* or "pleader" for the Jews had worked on an international problem. To add strength to their unity, the Jews soon joined together again under the leadership of Adolphe Cremieux, the brilliant French Jewish lawyer, to form the *Alliance Israelite Universelle*, The World Alliance of Jews, an international organization meant to protect the rights of Jews everywhere.

Still today the Alliance continues its work, serving Jews in Arab lands, and defending the rights of Jews throughout the world.

Hebrew and Arabic are taught side by side in this Alliance school in Morocco.

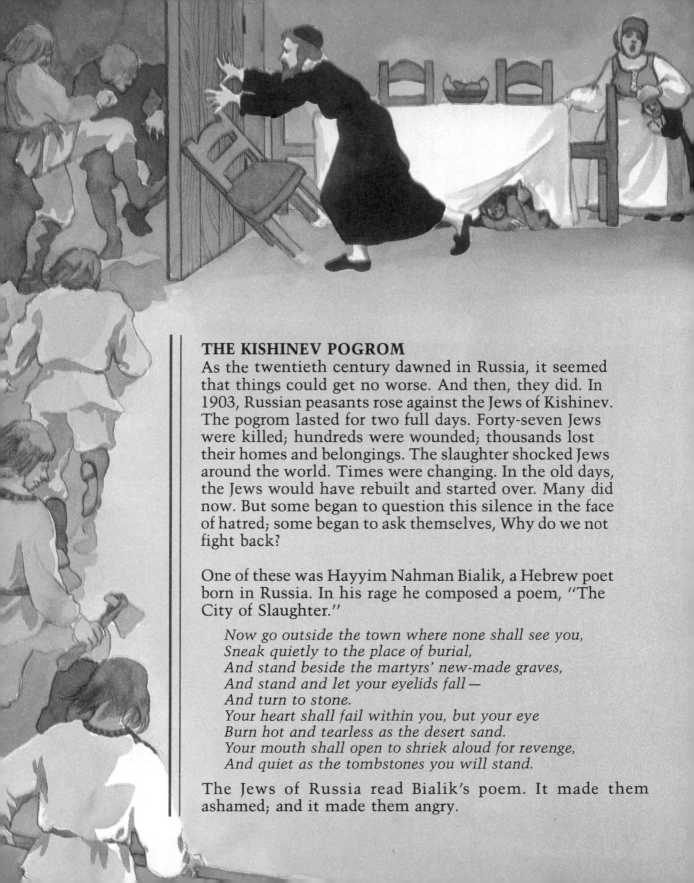

THE KISHINEV POGROM

As the twentieth century dawned in Russia, it seemed that things could get no worse. And then, they did. In 1903, Russian peasants rose against the Jews of Kishinev. The pogrom lasted for two full days. Forty-seven Jews were killed; hundreds were wounded; thousands lost their homes and belongings. The slaughter shocked Jews around the world. Times were changing. In the old days, the Jews would have rebuilt and started over. Many did now. But some began to question this silence in the face of hatred; some began to ask themselves, Why do we not fight back?

One of these was Hayyim Nahman Bialik, a Hebrew poet born in Russia. In his rage he composed a poem, "The City of Slaughter."

> *Now go outside the town where none shall see you,*
> *Sneak quietly to the place of burial,*
> *And stand beside the martyrs' new-made graves,*
> *And stand and let your eyelids fall—*
> *And turn to stone.*
> *Your heart shall fail within you, but your eye*
> *Burn hot and tearless as the desert sand.*
> *Your mouth shall open to shriek aloud for revenge,*
> *And quiet as the tombstones you will stand.*

The Jews of Russia read Bialik's poem. It made them ashamed; and it made them angry.

The Russian church (called the Orthodox church) made Jewish life even more uneasy by preaching hatred for the Jews. The church blamed the Jews for the miserable conditions of Russian peasant life. But, in truth, the Jews also were trapped, suffering the same kinds of conditions—and worse, for now the peasants turned against them, too.

Whatever small hopes the Jews of Russia and Poland had were crushed in 1881 when the czar that had been kindest to them, Alexander II, was murdered by revolutionaries. Alexander III blamed the Jews for the death of his father. From 1881 to 1883, *pogroms,* peasant riots against the Jews, occurred throughout Russia. Russian police stood by as Jews were murdered, as Jewish homes were burned and stores looted, as synagogues were destroyed and holy books dragged into the streets. Sometimes the police arrested Jews who tried to defend themselves.

The May Laws   It was during this period that Alexander signed a group of laws called the "May Laws" (signed in May 1882). Russian Jews—those who had been in Russia when the Pale of Settlement was set up—were now forced to move out of the large cities into the shtetls and small towns of the Pale. Almost 20,000 Jews were forced to leave Moscow alone. Jewish belongings and money were seized. Just to survive, nearly half of Russia's Jews needed charity.

Every anti-Jewish weapon was used against the Jews of Russia and Poland—even the blood libel. Under Nicholas, the son of Alexander III, a Jew named Beilis was accused of murdering a Christian boy for his blood. There was so little reason to find Beilis guilty that even the Russian court was at last forced to let him go—but not before poor Beilis had spent two years in the cold, damp darkness of a Russian prison cell.

For the Jews of Russia, it seemed that the whole Pale of Settlement was like that cold, damp, and dark cell; that they were all sentenced to suffer in it for life; and that the light of freedom shining in Europe and America would never find its way through the thick jail walls.

Mendel Beilis

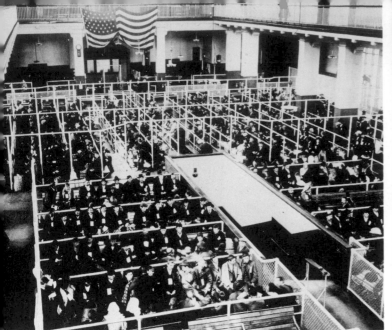

16 UPTOWN AND DOWNTOWN

Russian and other East European Jews fled to America in large numbers after 1881 when the anti-Jewish Czar Alexander III rose to power, a series of pogroms began, and the May Laws were signed. They stopped coming to America in 1914 when World War I made travel across Europe nearly impossible. It was the largest exodus, the greatest mass movement of Jews in history. In the thirty-four years of East European Jewish immigration, nearly 2,000,000 Jews arrived in the United States.

For the most part, the immigrants were poor. They came without jobs and without money, as the German Jews had done before them. But there were so many of them that it was difficult for the already settled German Jewish community to help them. In addition, the East European Jews seemed foreign, visitors from the past, reminders of the ghetto—and that made the German Jews uncomfortable. When the German Jews organized to help their new cousins, they did it in the way they thought best—giving money with one hand while trying to teach the East Europeans to be more like "American Jews" with the other. The East European Jews did not like that at all. To them, the Germans seemed strangers.

For one thing, it seemed that the German Jews behaved more like "Americans" than "Jews." They dressed in the

latest American fashions. They seldom wore *yarmulkes* (headcoverings); and many did not keep the Jewish laws of cooking and slaughtering (kashrut).

Also, a goodly number of the German Jews owned businesses and small factories. Not only did they work on the Sabbath, but they often asked their East European Jewish workers to do so, too! It seemed that the Jewish religion played little part in the lives of these German cousins; and the synagogues they prayed in and the way they behaved in them seemed as foreign to the Russian and East European Jews as the ways of the Russians were to the Germans.

Sweatshop and Union   During the Civil War, women and children were paid to turn pieces of blue material into uniforms for the Yankee soldiers. They often worked day and night, sewing and finishing in their homes. The Civil War ended, but the idea of using this kind of cheap labor did not. The East Europeans were willing to work long hours for small wages. And because of the large numbers of new Jewish immigrants there were never enough jobs. Workers making clothing crowded into close rooms filled with sewing machines, pressing irons, and racks of garments, with little air or light. If they complained, they were fired. New workers could be easily found. Worst of all,

Far left: Arriving at Ellis Island, Jews waited in long lines to answer questions, were quarantined, then finally allowed to enter the United States (photo, 1910). Center left: a Russian Jewish immigrant, 1900—his new life was ahead of him. Center right: Jews speak with authorities about emigration to America. Above: The clothing workers' strike in 1909—even the new life had its problems.

these "sweatshops" were often owned by the German Jews—so the fights were between Jewish bosses and Jewish laborers.

It was not long before the East European Jews tried to put an end to this struggle. One worker could not fight against a sweatshop owner, but if a whole shopful of workers united, the owner would have to listen or else go out of business. So the East Europeans formed labor unions. One of these, the International Ladies Garment Workers Union (ILGWU) went on strike against sweatshop owners in 1910. For two full months, over 60,000 ILGWU members refused to go to work. They wanted promises and action from the owners—shorter hours, better safety on the job, higher pay, more light and air, and just decent human treatment.

Louis D. Brandeis In 1908, two years before the strike, Louis D. Brandeis stood before the Supreme Court. He was not talking about law. He was telling the judges of the highest court in the land what it was like to be a woman in a sweatshop. He told them how many immigrants worked in these terrible places, how poorly they were paid, how many hours they were forced to labor, and how they suffered. Surely, he said, the United States should be able to pass new laws to force the owners to make sweatshops cleaner and work more bearable. Surely, the United States government should protect its citizens, keep them healthy, and guard their safety. The judges listened. What Brandeis said made sense. But should a government pass laws to tell owners how to run businesses? The vote was "yes"; Brandeis won his case.

Louis Dembitz Brandeis

And he kept on winning. He settled the long ILGWU strike of 1910 by bringing the two sides together and reminding them that being fair and just was a part of being Jewish. He believed in Zionism, so he helped raise money and win friends for the Jews of Palestine. And in 1916 he became the first Jew to serve as a judge on the Supreme Court. Though he was a German Jew, he gave of his energy to all Jews, seeking justice through the law.

Among the East Europeans   Some East European Jews imitated the German Jews. They opened small shops of their own, gave up their East European ways of dressing immediately, and kept their businesses open on the Sabbath. Sometimes they even owned sweatshops and employed other East European Jewish immigrants, treating them just as the German owners did.

The vast majority of East European Jews wished to build a new Jewish life in America. They opened hundreds of small synagogues or *shuls*, and trained their children in the *heder* (one-room schoolhouse) just as they had in the old country. They helped one another by setting up self-help organizations, one for each town or region in East Europe. These were called *landsmanshaften* (a *landsman* was a person who had been a neighbor in the old country). They settled close together in the crowded cities of Chicago, Philadelphia, and Baltimore—and by the hundreds of thousands on the Lower East Side of New York City.

They carried with them their writers and musicians, their actors and orators, and their own language—Yiddish. They set up newspapers in Yiddish, went to see plays written in Yiddish, listened for hours to Yiddish poets reciting, and read Yiddish books by writers like Sholem Aleichem, Mendele Mocher Seforim, and Y. L. Peretz.

Because so many of them lived in New York's Lower East Side, they came to be called the "Downtown Jews" by the Germans. And, in turn, they called the Germans "Uptown Jews." A distance separated them that was far greater than the short walk along New York City streets. It was the distance made up of two very different ways of life.

Striking workers of the ILGWU.

RELIGIOUS LIFE IN GERMANY

While German Jews were settling in the United States, changes were taking place in German Jewish life in Europe. The "official" Jewish community was being challenged by new leaders. Abraham Geiger and Samuel Holdheim tried to make Jewish practices more modern by shortening prayer services, adding choirs to sing some prayers, bringing organ music into the synagogue even on Shabbat, and giving sermons in German. Geiger called his new kind of Judaism, "Liberal"; Holdheim led a group called the *Reformgemeinde* (Association for Reform). When Geiger's ideas spread to England, the new movement there was called Liberal Judaism, but in America it was known as Reform Judaism. The reformers said that the teachings of the prophets were more important than customs and rituals such as kashrut and Shabbat. They said the "Mission of Israel" was to be a "lamp unto the nations," guiding other peoples in what is right and what is wrong.

In Frankfort, Germany, Rabbi Samson Raphael Hirsch taught that the commandments and rituals of Judaism could not be changed. Yet he believed that Jewish worship could be made more modern and beautiful, that the Bible could be studied in any language, and that the laws of nature were God's creation. This last was very important. Many Orthodox Jews thought science—the study of the laws of nature—was an enemy of Judaism. But Hirsch saw science as a part of God's laws. Hirsch's movement, called neo-Orthodoxy (New Orthodoxy), spread across Europe and into the New World.

The Germans who came to America in the mid-1800s found only synagogues run by Sephardi Jews, according to Sephardi customs. They built their own synagogues in which prayers were spoken in Ashkenazi Hebrew and the Ashkenazi prayer book was used. Some of these synagogues followed the movements of Holdheim and Geiger, and some the movement of Hirsch. But a few others followed a third movement that also came from Germany. This third movement was based on the teachings of Zechariah Frankel who said that giving up the laws of Judaism was "negative." What was needed was a "Positive Historical Judaism," which would change slowly, adding new laws to replace old ones, and always looking to the past for what it could teach us. In a way, his ideas were like those of Leopold Zunz (see chapter eleven) who had pioneered the "Science of Judaism" by his careful study of the past.

The "Positive Historical Judaism" of Frankel grew very slowly in America until the Russian Jews arrived in the late 1800s and early 1900s. Then it began to blossom and grow as it attracted large masses of Russian Jews. And by that time it was called Conservative Judaism because it tried to "conserve" the Jewish past even as it made changes to make Judaism more modern.

Samson Raphael Hirsch

Zechariah Frankel

Abraham Geiger

17 AMERICAN JEWS, AMERICAN JUDAISM

In Europe, where the church had been a part of the state, the Orthodox synagogue and its leaders often acted officially for the Jewish community in its dealings with the government. They were a sort of Jewish government, with courts of law, schools, and "official" synagogues. In the United States, where church and state were separated by law, each congregation was on its own, and most communities never united. In some ways this was good: Jews were free to choose any synagogue they wished—Reform, Conservative, or Orthodox; and no taxes were collected by the Jewish community. But there were drawbacks: Many Jews joined no synagogue at all; there were few trained rabbis—and none at all had been trained in the United States; and there was no control over kashrut, where controls were important to make sure that meat was slaughtered in a proper way and made kosher according to law. Also, without unity, no one could speak for the Jews on important questions. It was only natural that some Jewish religious leaders began to think in terms of unity.

Isaac Mayer Wise   Among the first to dream of one "American Judaism" was Rabbi Isaac Mayer Wise of Cincinnati, Ohio. He even composed a prayer book that he called *Minhag America*, "The American Ritual," and that he hoped all Jews in America could use. He shared his dream with other Jewish leaders, as well, especially with Isaac Leeser of Philadelphia, Pennsylvania. Leeser belonged to the Positive Historical (later the Conservative) movement; Wise was a Reform rabbi, born and trained in Europe. But, although they were both willing to make serious compromises to unite their two movements, the congregations around the country were not cooperative. And Wise turned his strength to building Reform Judaism.

He made important changes: counting women as a part of the minyan (the ten people Jewish law requires for public

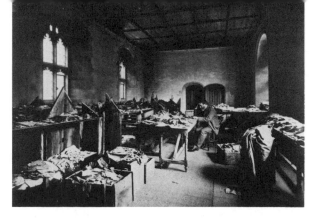

prayer) and allowing men and women to sit together during prayer. He founded Hebrew Union College in Cincinnati in 1875, training rabbis in America for the first time; and helped found the Union of American Hebrew Congregations and the Central Conference of American Rabbis, both of which united the Reform movement. He also edited two journals that brought Jewish news to readers across the country. His work made Reform Judaism the strongest movement in America for a time; and the leaders of the other movements studied what he had done and saw how they might make their movements stronger.

Solomon Schechter Conservative Judaism found its first real leader in Solomon Schechter who was brought to America in 1902 to become the head of the new Jewish Theological Seminary in New York. Schechter was already world famous. He had discovered the Cairo genizah. A genizah is a place where holy books, often tattered and torn into fragments, are placed when they become worn. Schechter heard that there was a genizah in Cairo's ancient synagogue, and he traveled to see it for himself. He returned to England with 100,000 manuscripts and fragments to study—the richest find of manuscripts in modern times. Among the fragments was one that brought him fame—the Book of Ben Sira, mentioned in ancient writings, but lost for centuries.

At first, Schechter—like Wise and Leeser—tried to unite all American Jews. When this failed, he worked to make Conservative Judaism strong by making the Seminary strong. He brought great scholars to teach the young Conservative rabbis, and built one of the world's finest Jewish libraries. In 1909, he opened a Teacher's Institute to train Jewish teachers

Solomon Schechter actually *re*-discovered the Cairo Genizah. Many fragments had been brought out by other scholars before him, but he arranged for the entire Genizah to be removed to England. When he came to America, he brought many of these fragments across the ocean to continue studying them. Not only the Jews, but their books and their belongings, have been great world travellers. Right: Isaac Mayer Wise.

and made Rabbi Mordecai M. Kaplan, a Seminary graduate, its first head.

Toward the end of his life, Schechter founded the United Synagogue, bringing all Conservative congregations into one union; and, shortly after he died, the Rabbinical Assembly was formed to unite graduates of the Seminary. By refusing to give up tradition except where necessary, and by combining serious study of the past with change for the future (the Science of Judaism), Schechter built what would become America's largest Jewish movement.

Jacob Joseph of Vilna   The problems of Orthodox Judaism in America were so great that many European rabbis, looking on from afar, called America "the *trefah* land," the land where nothing is kosher. There were few trained Orthodox rabbis in America, while the number of Orthodox congregations was growing. What was sold by butchers as "kosher" meat, was not always really kosher; and with no organization in control, it was hard to know what was and what was not kosher. Finally fifteen Orthodox congregations in New York formed a union in 1879 to choose a "chief rabbi." They searched for nine years among the rabbis of Eastern Europe until they found one, Rabbi Jacob Joseph of Vilna, who was willing to come to America. Even before Jacob Joseph arrived, the unity of the Orthodox community began to dissolve. Some congregations had changed their minds about wanting a single leader. Nor could enough money be raised to pay the salary that had been promised to Jacob Joseph. The union itself fell apart, and the idea of having a "chief rabbi" (even when it was tried by the Jews of other cities) never worked.

In a way, it was more difficult for the Orthodox congregations to unite. First, there were so many congregations, and so few good leaders. Second, the Orthodox Jews came from so many different places—Russia, Poland, Rumania, Lithuania, Austria, Hungary, Galicia, Germany and each group still followed its own folkways and traditions, though all followed the Shulhan Aruch, the Torah, and the Talmud. Yet the need for unity was great, and it could not be put off forever. In 1898, many congregations joined the Union of Orthodox Jewish Congregations; and afterward Orthodox rabbis formed several unions: the Union of Orthodox Rabbis, the Rabbinical Council of America, and (for Hasidic rabbis) the Central Rabbinical Congress.

A New Unity   A new kind of Jewish unity had been created in America, a unity of movements and not of communities. Though it was different from the unity Jews had in Europe, it was better suited to life in North America. Slowly the three movements became settled and established, and even for the Orthodox, America became more "kosher" and less "trefah."

YESHIVA UNIVERSITY

For a long while, rabbis of Orthodox Judaism in America came only from the great schools (yeshivot) of Talmud learning in the old country. Then, in 1896, a yeshivah for the study of Talmud was founded in New York to train young Orthodox rabbis. Twelve years later, the students asked to be allowed to study secular subjects as well—history, mathematics, and science. And these subjects were joined to the study of Talmud for the first time. In 1915, Dr. Bernard Revel became head of the yeshivah and added a high school division, a school to train Jewish teachers, and a four-year college. Yeshiva University continued to grow, adding more schools: a college of medicine, a women's division called Stern College, and a school of social work. In time a West Coast branch was opened. Now in truth the ideas of Samson Raphael Hirsch had come to America: Torah and Talmud were being taught side by side with modern knowledge.

TRAINING RABBIS AND LEADERS

In places like Philadelphia, Chicago, Baltimore, and Boston, colleges to train Jewish teachers and teach Jewish subjects were set up. In addition, the Orthodox founded many yeshivot to teach Talmud and Torah as they had been taught in Europe. In 1922, Rabbi Stephen S. Wise, a champion both of labor and of Zionism, founded the Jewish Institute of Religion in New York City to train rabbis for all movements, but most of the graduates joined the Reform movement. In time, the Jewish Institute of Religion merged with Hebrew Union College of Cincinnati. Two other branches were opened, one in Los Angeles and one in Jerusalem. The Jewish Theological Seminary also opened a school in Los Angeles (the University of Judaism) and a center for Conservative Judaism in Israel. The Orthodox set up a Yeshiva University of Los Angeles, too, just as there was a Yeshiva University in New York City.

From the 1920s on, Hillel Foundations on college campuses around the country gave Jewish university students a place to meet, pray, and study together when prejudices often kept them from joining college fraternities and sororities. Brandeis University, named for the Supreme Court judge, was founded in Massachusetts in 1948 as a place where Jews could study with non-Jews without facing the prejudice they sometimes met elsewhere. And, in the 1960s, many state and private universities in the United States added courses and departments of Jewish studies to serve their students.

Left: The Hebrew Union College-Jewish Institute of Religion in Cincinnati.
Right: The Jewish Theological Seminary of America in New York.

18 THE BIRTH OF ZIONISM

In the 1800s an idea was planted like a small seed in the mind of the Jewish people. It took root in the Jewish tradition's "Love of Zion"; but it also borrowed from a movement in nations like France, Germany, England, and Austria called *Nationalism.*

Nationalism is the belief that each people or "nation" should speak its own language, live in its own land, make its own laws, and follow its own culture. Some Jewish thinkers began to speak of "Jewish nationalism." Jews, they said, already had most of what was needed: We are one people. The Torah contains our law. We have a language of our own. And we have a strong culture, a tradition to live by. What we do not have at present, they said, is a land of our own.

But we know what land it is, for we have always remembered our "Love of Zion." In the Torah, God promised the

The BILU chose Pinsker as their leader in a secret meeting that marked the beginning of the movement to Israel.

Jews a land—the land of Israel—to be forever theirs. And, though the majority of the Jewish people had been separated from this land for many generations, there was no time in history when they had not spoken of it, prayed to be returned to it, visited it on pilgrimages, written of it, and even gone to live in it. In fact, there was no time since Joshua led the people of Israel across the Jordan River when Jews had not been living in Israel (or, as it was called by others, Palestine). Despite the hardships of life in a land that had few natural resources, little business and trade, and a population made up in large part of Arabs and many small Christian religious groups, Jews had always considered living in Israel to be a *mitzvah* ("religious duty"). Life outside Israel was incomplete; and there were many commandments that could only be observed if one lived in the Holy Land.

Now Jewish nationalism and Love of Zion gained strength in Russia, where the Jews were suffering most. While many Russian Jews were leaving for countries like England, South Africa, Argentina, and the United States, some began to question the wisdom of such movement. Even in these countries of freedom, they thought, there is still hatred of the Jews. The only place where Jews could be truly safe and free from persecution, they said, would be in a land of our own. Only in our own country could we live full lives as Jews. And that country had to be Zion, the Holy Land, the land God promised to the Israelites in the Covenant.

Hovevei Zion   Small groups of Jews in Russia met to talk about this idea. They began the movement called *Hovevei Zion,* the "Lovers of Zion." At first, they met secretly. They knew that their idea of Jewish nationalism was shocking to most Jews. For thousands of years, Jewish tradition had taught that God would return the Jews to the Promised Land when the time was right. Going too soon would be like "forcing God's hand," and that was forbidden. Yet that was precisely what the Hovevei Zion had in mind. And that was what they discussed endlessly in their small groups. But, as yet, no single force had united them or called them to action.

It was a book that finally spoke out for them. In 1881 as pogroms broke out in 160 cities in Russia, a sixty-year-old physician in Odessa began writing. His name was Leon Pinsker; and the book he wrote was called *Self-Emancipation.* It was time, Pinsker stated boldly, for the Jews to set *themselves* free. And he quoted the words of the ancient sage Hillel: "If I am not for myself, who will be for me? . . . And if not now, when?"

From the moment *Self-Emancipation* appeared in 1882, the Hovevei Zion knew that they had found a voice. Using Pinsker's work to gain new members for the movement, the leaders called for a first national conference in 1884. A few even dared to take action by leaving for Palestine. The seed of Zionism was growing.

Theodor Herzl   In 1896, a Jewish newspaperman and playwright, Theodor Herzl, wrote a book called *The Jewish State.* Herzl lived in Vienna, Austria. He had never read Pinsker's book, yet his ideas were much the same. The difference was that Herzl, unlike Pinsker, was himself a person of action. He called on Jews to gather together to create a Jewish nation.

It was like a miracle. In answer to his call, 200 leading Jews from all parts of the world came to Basle, Switzerland in the summer of 1897 for a Zionist Congress. Herzl insisted that the delegates dress formally for this grand occasion. The delegates wore top hats and tuxedos to the sessions of the Congress (even the poorer East European delegates were given formal suits to wear). The movement of Zionism was born.

Theodor Herzl

The Zionist Congress declared that it would seek "to secure for the Jewish people" a "home in Palestine." An international organization was created called the World Zionist Organization; and Herzl was made its head.

Theodor Herzl spent the rest of his life speaking, writing,

THE DREYFUS TRIAL

Theodor Herzl said it was the Dreyfus trial more than any other event that convinced him of the need for Zionism. His newspaper sent him to Paris to report on that trial. But he hardly expected at the time, that the trial of a military captain accused of being a spy would change his life!

Captain Alfred Dreyfus was an assimilated French Jew—so assimilated, in fact, that he knew very little about his people and its history. He was a career officer, devoted to the French government. Now he was falsely accused of having sold French army secrets to the Germans. After an unfair trial, the innocent Dreyfus was sentenced to life imprisonment on Devil's Island.

Herzl was among the reporters watching the ceremony in which Dreyfus was publicly dishonored before being sent to the island prison. As the crowd began to yell, Herzl was shocked. The crowd was not just yelling, "Down with the traitor!" or "Down with the spy!" They were yelling, "Down with the Jews!" Suddenly Herzl realized that no country—not even France, the birthplace of the Age of Reason and one of the first to grant Jews equal rights—was free of its age-old prejudices.

Dreyfus was later proved innocent and released from Devil's Island; he was another of history's innocent victims. Herzl went on to become one of Jewish history's great heroes.

and working for the Jewish homeland. And because he was a person of action, he counted on his dream to come true. Today, every schoolchild in Israel knows by heart Herzl's famous saying, "If you will it, it is no dream!" Herzl wished a Jewish state for his people and, while others thought it was only a dream, he always believed it was a vision of the future. With his help, the seed of Zionism has become a tree of life for the Jews.

The Tree Grows Branches The Jewish people are like a family. Inside our home, in private, we argue. We have always argued—about almost everything. The Pharisees argued with the Sadducees. Hillel argued with Shammai. The Hasidim argued with the Mitnaggedim. The Reformers argued with the Orthodox. Yet, we remain one family. In the Talmud, such arguments are given a lovely name. They are called, "arguments for the sake of Heaven," because such arguments are healthy. They help us grow by forcing us to think clearly about what we believe.

From the very first, the Zionist movement was full of arguments. Some—even Herzl, for a while—felt that the need of the Russian Jews for safety was so great that any country could serve as a temporary Jewish homeland. Most, especially the Russian Jews, believed that only the Holy Land could be the Jewish home. Some thought the Jews should go

Left: Basle, Switzerland, where Herzl convened the First Zionist Congress in 1897.

Right: A journalist's painting of Herzl at the Second Zionist Congress.

A class portrait: In the center of this group of agricultural students is David Ben Gurion who would later become the first Prime Minister of Israel.

Right: At a conference in 1945, Rabbi Stephen S. Wise presented Herzl's ring to Chaim Weizmann, soon to become the first President of Israel.

to the Holy Land immediately; buy parcels of it and farm them. Some thought that the governments of the world should first proclaim that the land belonged to the Jews. Some believed that the new homeland would be Jewish only if it followed traditional Jewish law, *halachah*. Others believed that the new land would need new laws. Some said that all Jews should come to the new homeland. Others said that the Holy Land could serve as the center of Jewish life even while most Jews continued to live outside of it, in the Diaspora.

Soon, the Zionist movement was made up of many smaller groups, each with its own ideas. There was political Zionism, cultural Zionism, religious Zionism, labor Zionism, secular Zionism, and so on. After the State of Israel was formed, each group became a political party, so that Israel today has many different parties. It seems that politicians there, more so than in most countries, are constantly arguing and disagreeing.

Yet all these parties basically agree that theirs should be "arguments for the sake of Heaven," that is, arguments that seek to unify and not to divide the Jews of Israel. And the Zionist movement has also helped to keep the Jews of the world united in modern times, so that even today we can say we are *am ehad*, "One People."

BILU AND THE FIRST ALIYAH

Aliyah means "going up." The Hebrew word is used for the honor of being called to take part in the Torah reading in a synagogue. It is also used for "going up" to Israel, to settle there. In modern times, each wave of immigration to Israel has been called an aliyah. The First Aliyah lasted from 1882 to 1903. By the end, about 25,000 Jews had settled in Palestine. Officially, the First Aliyah began in July 1882, when fourteen members of Hovevei Zion made the hard journey from Russia to the Holy Land. They called themselves BILU,בילו, using the initial letters of בית יעקוב, לכו ונלכה, "O House of Jacob, come and let us go up."

Life in Palestine at the turn of the century was grim. At first, to learn farming, the BILU members worked eleven and twelve hours a day in an Alliance farm school (see page 121). Then they were given a small piece of land. They called their new settlement *Rishon le-tzion*, "First to Zion." But the harvest season had nearly passed, and their plantings of corn and vegetables did not grow. Six of the fourteen, broken in spirit and exhausted, returned to Russia. The rest faced diseases that spread from the swamps, the heat of the burning sun, and the loss of their cattle to Bedouin Arab raiders. Yet they held on; and soon hundreds more came to settle.

Help came, too, from the French Jewish banker, Baron Edmond de Rothschild. He sent money, and he also sent farming experts who taught the settlers how to grow grapes and set up wineries. In return for his help, Rothschild asked only that his name be kept a secret. So, for many years, the settlers (who knew the secret) spoke only of *Ha-Nadiv Ha-Yadua*, "the well-known, generous one." Even with all the help, it was a slow beginning. It took three years for the first good harvest of grapes; and then the wine had to be fermented and aged. But it was a beginning.

For the BILU, life was tough. They often took cold, meagre meals in the fields as they worked (photo, left); and the number of the survivors—seen in the photo at right—after the first year was small.

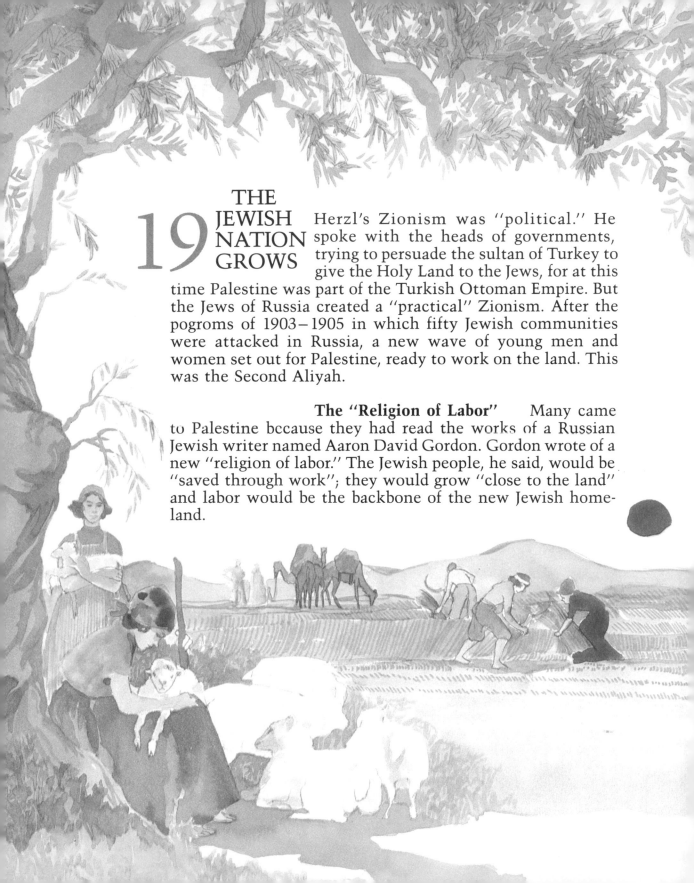

19 THE JEWISH NATION GROWS

Herzl's Zionism was "political." He spoke with the heads of governments, trying to persuade the sultan of Turkey to give the Holy Land to the Jews, for at this time Palestine was part of the Turkish Ottoman Empire. But the Jews of Russia created a "practical" Zionism. After the pogroms of 1903–1905 in which fifty Jewish communities were attacked in Russia, a new wave of young men and women set out for Palestine, ready to work on the land. This was the Second Aliyah.

The "Religion of Labor" Many came to Palestine because they had read the works of a Russian Jewish writer named Aaron David Gordon. Gordon wrote of a new "religion of labor." The Jewish people, he said, would be "saved through work"; they would grow "close to the land" and labor would be the backbone of the new Jewish homeland.

Gordon's ideas of the "religion of labor" gave hope and promise to the difficult task of redeeming the land and making it fertile again.

In 1904, Gordon himself came to Palestine. Soon he joined a "collective settlement," a *kibbutz.* On the kibbutz, everyone worked together, and all shared equally whatever was produced. They had no need for money on the kibbutz. There was nothing there to buy. If a person wanted something—a new shirt, a pair of trousers—and it was in the storeroom, then that person just took it. People on the kibbutz, called *kibbutzniks,* worked and lived and played as if they were one family. Children, even babies, lived apart from their parents in special houses where nurses and teachers looked after them. Following work, they would visit with their parents; and after dinner return to the children's house. Men and women shared equally. Women often worked in the fields, men worked in the laundries and kitchens. At harvest time, everyone worked in the fields.

When Gordon arrived at Kibbutz Deganyah, he was already forty-eight years old. Most of the settlers were much younger—in their twenties, even in their teens. He seemed an old man to them. Yet he worked with them all day long in the fields, he led the dancing around the campfires at night, and he stayed up until the early hours of the morning, studying and writing. With Gordon's leadership and help, Deganyah became a model for other settlements, and soon there were many *kibbutzim.* The religion of labor, and labor Zionism, gained strength. Jews were at last becoming farmers.

Aaron David Gordon

The Rebirth of Hebrew   Back in Russia, the Hebrew language was being used for modern purposes. Poets like Bialik composed their poetry in Hebrew. Famous thinkers like Ahad ha-Am—his real name was Asher Ginsberg and the pen name he chose means "One of the People"—wrote for Hebrew newspapers and magazines. There had been a movement in Russia called the Haskalah. This was not the Haskalah of Mendelssohn that had tried to teach Jews to live as modern Germans. In Russia, it was a movement to spread new learning and modern ideas through the use of the Hebrew language. Yet the *Maskilim* ("enlighteners"—from the word *haskalah*) did not *speak* Hebrew in their everyday lives. So, although, many of the Jews who came to Palestine in the Second Aliyah had studied some Hebrew, few were able to speak it.

As a matter of fact, for a while it seemed that Yiddish or German, or perhaps even Russian, might become the everyday language of the Jews in Palestine. Except for the work of one family.

It happened almost by chance. A Jewish medical student in Paris met a Jewish reporter and they talked. The reporter told of a trip to Asia and Africa, and of meeting Jews in these faraway places. Since the reporter could not speak the languages of these countries, he spoke to the Jews there in the Holy Tongue (Hebrew was called that since it was used mainly for prayer and Bible study, not for common conversation). The medical student, Eliezer Ben-Yehudah, was amazed and excited. Coming from an Orthodox Hasidic family, he too had studied Hebrew—but he had not imagined speaking it. Now he wrote to Deborah, his future wife,

> *I have decided that . . . we need a language to hold us together. That language is Hebrew, but not the Hebrew of the rabbis and scholars. We must have a language in which we can conduct business.*

Soon after, Eliezer and Deborah were married. When Eliezer took sick with tuberculosis, they decided to move to the dry climate of Palestine for his health. And aboard the ship bound for the Holy Land they swore to one another that they would speak only Hebrew together for the rest of their lives—and so they did. Their children were the first in modern times to grow up in a home where no language but Hebrew was spoken.

Eliezer ben Yehudah and his family devoted their lives to the revival of spoken Hebrew.

TEL AVIV

Most Jews who came in the First Aliyah or the Second
Aliyah entered Palestine through the port of Jaffa—and
many stayed, just as many who arrived in America
through the port of New York stayed there. Jaffa became
overcrowded and cramped; its streets were too narrow
for the heavy traffic caused by the newcomers. Finally, in
1909, sixty families decided to build "garden houses"
away from Jaffa, in a place where they could live quietly.
They named their new settlement *Tel Aviv*, Hill of
Spring—the Hebrew title of a novel by Theodor Herzl.

Tel Aviv did not remain a garden city for long. Streets
with names like Herzl, Ahad ha-Am, Judah Halevi, and
Rothschild soon filled up with new immigrants. What
made it different was that it was a Jewish city, the first
modern all-Jewish city. For a while, Tel Aviv was the
national capital of Israel. Today, it is Israel's busiest city:
its Dizengoff Square is famous throughout the country as
a place for shopping and meeting friends, it is the center
of the large diamond industry of Israel, and the center of
Labor Zionism. In fact, Tel Aviv is so modern that it has
all the problems of modern cities everywhere—noise,
overcrowding, crime, and pollution. Yet, like all great
cities, Tel Aviv is a center for music, dance, theater,
museums, and libraries. In other words, it is a city filled
with life.

The importance of what Eliezer ben Yehudah, Hemdah Ben-Yehudah, and their children accomplished is deep. Hebrew unites Jews throughout the world and throughout the centuries. After all, a family must share a language.

Eliezer agreed to teach in an Alliance school in Jerusalem, but only if he could teach in Hebrew. Soon he convinced other teachers to use Hebrew in their classrooms. When a new college, the Technion, was opened in Haifa, it was decided that classes there would be taught in German, the language of modern science. Eliezer argued with the people at the college. They said that Hebrew was not useful because many of the words needed by modern science were new—there was not even a Hebrew word for railroad! Eliezer said that new words could be created, what was truly important was that Hebrew should be the language of the Jews. All over the country teachers went out on strike to support Eliezer; and at last the Technion people agreed to use only Hebrew at the new college. This was the great turning point.

Already the *halutzim* ("pioneers"—this was the name by which the people of the Second Aliyah called one another) were practicing Hebrew day by day as they worked in the fields or sang around the campfires. And now most of the schools were teaching in Hebrew as well. Only the Orthodox were still opposed to the rebirth of spoken Hebrew. They continued to believe that Hebrew was too holy for everyday use. A few Jews in Israel today still believe this, and continue to speak and teach in Yiddish—but thanks to Eliezer and Hemdah, Hebrew became the language of the Jewish homeland.

Eliezer went on to compile a huge dictionary of the Hebrew language, creating many new words. Hemdah wrote books in Hebrew. It almost seems a miracle that spoken Hebrew was reborn, but think what it means to us today: Hebrew is the key to Jewish writing and thinking of all times and places—and every schoolchild in Israel now can tap untold treasures from the Jewish past, just because Hebrew is the language of Israel!

The Shomerim One great problem faced by the halutzim was self-defense. At night, gangs of Arab horsemen would break into the Jewish farms and kibbutzim, stealing cattle and food, and attacking the Jews. Since the time of the First Aliyah, the Jews had been hiring local Arabs to guard their town gates at night, but often these "guards" were the ones who threw open the gates for the raiders! At last, young leaders like David Ben-Gurion and Isaac Ben-Zvi organized a group called *Ha-Shomer*, "The Guard." Buying weapons and learning to use them, the Jewish *Shomerim* ("guards") hired themselves out to the kibbutzim and settlements to guard the gates. When the Arabs came, the Shomerim fought against them; and soon the raiders learned that the Jews could protect themselves.

The people of the Second Aliyah were learning a new trade—farming—at the same time they were studying a new language—Hebrew—and at the same time they were training to protect themselves. Outside of Palestine it was often said that the Jews in the Holy Land used their left arms to plow while they used their right arms to carry weapons. They still suffered at times from malaria that spread from the swamps; and their lives were made dangerous by the frequent night raids. But their spirits were high. They were building a new nation, a homeland. Inch by inch, and side by side, they were working toward a new life for themselves and for all the Jewish people.

Left: They called themselves "pioneers," and they took their task seriously. The land they farmed turned green and bore fruit, across the road it was often barren and wild. Right: Being a pioneer could even mean feeding the ducks and turkeys.

The Balfour Declaration as illuminated by Arthur Szyk, a prominent modern Jewish artist. Coming in 1917, it gave hope and promise to a Jewish dream of independence.

THE BALFOUR DECLARATION

The Second Aliyah brought nearly 40,000 East European Jews to Palestine. "Practical" Zionism was beginning to succeed. Then, in 1914, World War I broke out in Europe; and the immigration stopped. The English, fighting against the Ottoman Turks, hoped that the Jews of Palestine would support the English cause. So "political" Zionism began to work.

Its foremost leader was Russian-born, but now lived and worked in England. He was Chaim Weizmann, a Jewish scientist who turned his skills toward helping the British in their war efforts. Partly as a reward for his help, and partly to gain the favor of the Jews of Palestine, the British government decided that the time was ripe to give the Zionists what they wanted most. In 1917, the head of the British Foreign Office, Lord Balfour, sent a copy of an official letter to Lord Rothschild. In it, England promised to help create a Jewish homeland in Palestine. Zionists everywhere rejoiced over this letter, the "Balfour Declaration." For the first time, the dream of a Jewish homeland guaranteed by a world power seemed possible.

Just as the British had hoped, the Zionists now did what they could to ensure that England would defeat the Turks. Weizmann even helped to form a Jewish army corps to join the British army. It was the first official Jewish fighting force since the time of the Bar Kochba Revolt.

In the center of this photograph, standing, is Lord Balfour. Seated, below and just to his right, is Chaim Weizmann.

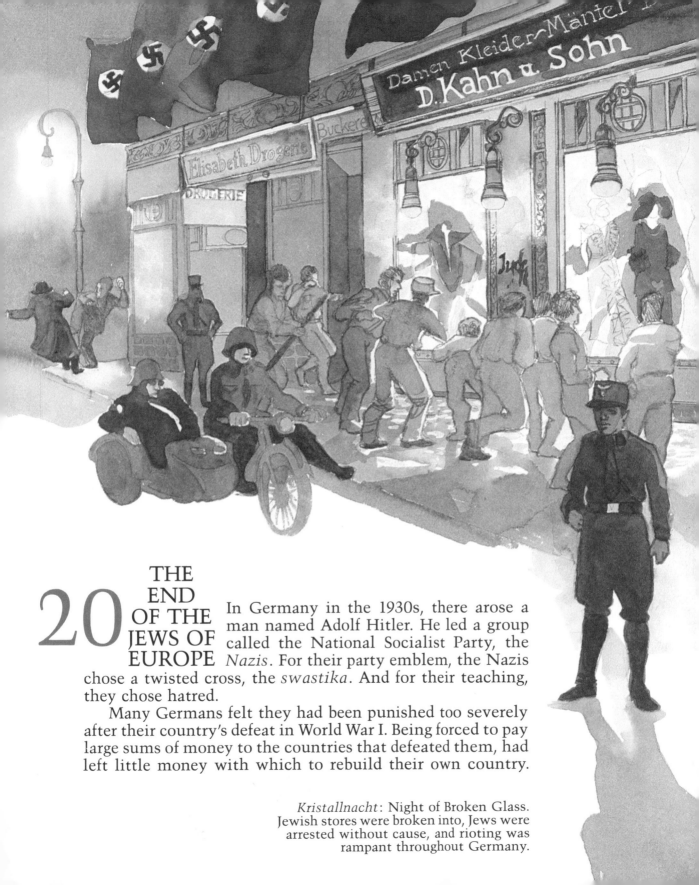

20 THE END OF THE JEWS OF EUROPE

In Germany in the 1930s, there arose a man named Adolf Hitler. He led a group called the National Socialist Party, the *Nazis*. For their party emblem, the Nazis chose a twisted cross, the *swastika*. And for their teaching, they chose hatred.

Many Germans felt they had been punished too severely after their country's defeat in World War I. Being forced to pay large sums of money to the countries that defeated them, had left little money with which to rebuild their own country.

Kristallnacht: Night of Broken Glass. Jewish stores were broken into, Jews were arrested without cause, and rioting was rampant throughout Germany.

Then in 1929, the Great Depression struck—an economic catastrophe in which banks closed, stocks and bonds became worthless, and many people lost their lifetime savings. It was this way in England and France and the United States, as well as in Germany. But in most countries, people began slowly to rebuild. In Germany, the leaders were weak and could not agree on a plan for rebuilding.

For the weak Germans, Hitler explained everything. They were weak, he said, because they had been betrayed by their leaders and by the Jews. Really, Hitler said, the Germans—members of the so-called "Aryan Race"—should be the "Master Race," rulers of the world. To become world rulers, the Germans would have to turn against those who were not Aryans, people of other races, especially peoples like the Jews—who, he claimed, were members of an "inferior" race, the Semites. This doctrine was known as "racism," the notion that some races were superior to others; and the old prejudices against the Jews were given a new name, *anti-Semitism*. Hitler set all his ideas down in a book called *Mein Kampf*, "My Struggle."

Hitler in Germany   Hitler launched his anti-Semitic program as soon as he came into power in 1933. Laws were passed forbidding Germans to buy things from Jews, to use the services of Jewish doctors and lawyers. Jewish professors and teachers were forbidden to teach non-Jews. Later, Jews were forbidden to attend universities. Newspapers and magazines published articles showing that the Jews were "less than human," and German children read this in their schoolbooks. Jewish books were burned and forbidden. On the night of November 9, 1938, the Nazis and their followers attacked and destroyed almost every synagogue in Germany. Nearly 30,000 Jews were arrested; Jewish stores were looted and burned. It was called the "Night of Broken Glass," in German *Kristallnacht*, and it shattered the hopes of Germany's Jews forever.

Top: A Jew is arrested in Berlin. Center: Mass rallies were held to teach hatred. Bottom: Synagogues were desecrated.

JEWISH RESISTANCE

When they could, Jews in Europe fought back against the
Nazis. Few in number, they often joined non-Jewish
"underground" movements (except in Poland, where the
members of the Polish underground were themselves
anti-Semites). And sometimes, often when it was almost
too late, whole ghettos fought back when the Germans
came to round up Jews and send them to the death
camps. For example, almost 450,000 Jews had already
been sent from the Warsaw ghetto to their deaths when
the last 60,000 Jews determined to fight. Nevertheless,
the Jewish resistance at Warsaw was fierce. With small
weapons they had smuggled into the ghetto, and with
whatever weapons they could steal from the Germans,
the Jews held off German tanks and cannon for
twenty-eight days. In the end, most were captured or
killed; the Warsaw ghetto was burned and reduced to
ruins. But Hitler's army had paid a high price for this
small victory.

Resistance with guns was not often possible. Most Jews
fought back in a different way. Like the great rabbi, Leo
Baeck, who refused to leave his community and was sent
to Theresienstadt; and the great teacher, Janusz Korczak
who insisted on marching off to death with the children
he had taught, the Jews fought back by keeping their
faith alive. Teaching and studying, presenting plays,
writing histories, holding Passover seders and
celebrating Shabbat as best they could—the Jews
resisted. As desperate as the Jewish prisoners became,
even in the death camps, almost none of them
committed suicide. Most lived in hope, believing that
Germany would be defeated in time, wanting to survive
to tell the truth about what had happened, demanding
with their every breath that it never happen again.

Left: Jews arriving at Buchenwald, one of the Nazi camps. Center: The Austrian troops forced Jewish children to labor long hours cleaning the streets in Galicia. Right: Line-up in a concentration camp. It was impossible to know if this would be the last line-up—if the inmates would now be sent to the death camps to be gassed, or if they would be sent back to their barracks.

The War In 1939, Hitler's armies invaded and conquered Poland. World War II began. In nearly every country the Germans conquered, the Jews were forced to wear yellow stars on their clothing and to live in ghettos as they had in the Middle Ages. Jews from countries like Belgium and France were shipped by train to ghettos in the East. Where a few thousand had lived before, hundreds and hundreds of thousands of Jews were now crowded together. There was never enough food; diseases spread; people trying to escape or to smuggle food across the ghetto walls were shot. In winter, people froze to death in the cold; all year long, people died of hunger in the streets. Even so, the Jews of the ghettos continued to teach and study, to write and think. They tried to keep alive their Jewish ways, living as best they could, helping one another as much as possible. They did not lose hope and even as things grew worse they refused to believe that the world would forget them.

When the Nazis invaded Russia in 1941, they set out to destroy the Jewish community there. Nazi soldiers led Jewish families into the forests, forced them to dig huge ditches, stripped them of clothing and jewelry, and then shot them and threw their bodies into the ditches. In one such place, Babi Yar, over 10,000 Jews were murdered and buried. The Jews were unarmed and unprepared. They were helpless against the might of the German armies.

The Death Camps France had been conquered; England was weakening. It seemed that Russia might soon fall. Hitler and his top Nazi leaders grew bolder. They looked for a "Final Solution" to what they called "the Jewish problem." When they saw that no one spoke out against the murder of the Jews, they set out to murder even more of them—all of them if they could. In 1942, they ordered that death camps be set up all over Europe.

When the Jews arrived in the death camps, they were divided into two groups. Strong Jews were allowed to live a while, to work. The old, the sick, the young, and most women were sent to the "showers." But there was no water—only poison gas. The naked Jews were pressed closely together, the doors were locked, and when the doors opened again, there were the dead and the smell of gas. Everything of value was taken from the corpses—even gold teeth. And what remained was burned in huge ovens. Even those who had lived to work died within a few months. In one camp, Auschwitz, over 2,000,000 Jews were murdered in this way; 500,000 more died of starvation and disease. They had been

The Holocaust
1941 to 1945

—— International Borders 1937
□ Extermination Camps
■ Major Concentration Camps

Upper number – the population before 1941
Lower number – the population after 1945

North Sea

SWEDEN

DENMARK
6,000
5,900

Baltic Sea

LATVIA
100,000
30,000

LITHUANIA
140,000
36,000

EAST PRUSSIA

140,000
36,000
HOLLAND

250,000
70,000
GERMANY

POLAND
□ **3,000,000**
400,000

Atlantic Ocean

BELGIUM
85,000
57,000

81,000
21,000
CZECHOSLOVAKIA

OCCUPIED RUSSIA
2,500,000
1,750,000

FRANCE
300,000
235,000

SWITZER LAND

70,000
10,000
AUSTRIA

710,000
510,000
HUNGARY

1,000,000
250,000
RUMANIA

ITALY
120,000
111,000

70,000
12,000
YUGOSLAVIA

Black Sea

Mediterranean Sea

ALBANIA

48,000
8,000
BULGARIA

67,000
7,000
GREECE

0   100 200 300 400 miles

Ascherl

citizens of Holland, Belgium, France, Poland, Hungary, Czechoslovakia, Greece, and other countries. They were given no trial; they were shown no mercy, they had done nothing wrong; they were put to death for being Jewish.

The Nazi Crime   As he slowly rose to power, few had taken Hitler seriously. Many thought he was just another politician. He will never keep his promises, they said. Not his good promises and not his threats. In the end, he failed to keep his promises to make the Germans the masters of the world. But he did keep almost every evil vow he had made. He spread hatred into the hearts of Germans, destroyed most of the Gypsies of Europe, turned Germans against one another with his secret police (the SS and the SD), looted and robbed all the great cities of Europe, and murdered millions of Russians even as millions more died of starvation; and he destroyed the faith of the world in the goodness of human beings. And he kept the most evil vow he had made: in the most gruesome crime ever committed against human beings, the Holocaust, the Nazis murdered 6,000,000 innocent Jews—men, women, and children—just because they were Jews.

"Beds" in the camps. The Nazis planned carefully to be sure that the treatment of the Jews was always as brutal as possible.

When Jewish communities living outside of German rule heard of this murdering, they protested to their governments. The governments told them that it was more important to fight the war and to defeat the German armies than to concentrate on the sufferings of Europe's Jews. But the fighting of the war went on for years while nothing was done to stop the awful slaughter of the Jews—and, in the end, nearly one-third of world Jewry had been destroyed.

Years after Hitler and the Nazis had been defeated in 1945, long after the few survivors of the death camps were freed, Jews around the world still wondered: Did we do enough to stop the horror? Could we have done more?

And the Jewish people made a new covenant, never to let it happen again, never to be silent when Jews anywhere are in danger, never to stand idly by while Jews are being murdered.

THE RIGHTEOUS GENTILES

In the dark years of the Holocaust, there are few bright moments. Some Gentiles, non-Jews, helped by hiding Jewish friends. Priests and nuns sometimes helped by hiding Jewish children. Though the churches were silent, some ministers spoke out against the Nazis. But for most Jews there was no help; and no place to go.

In Denmark it was different. Though the Nazis ruled there, the Danes refused to obey anti-Jewish laws. The king of Denmark, Christian X, told the Germans that if the Jews were forced to wear yellow stars, he and all his people would wear them, too. Even so, in 1943, the Germans decided to send the Jews of Denmark to the death camps. When the Danes learned of this, they helped the Jews escape. Day and night they sailed their small fishing boats loaded with Jewish friends and neighbors across the channel—past the German gun boats—to free Sweden. Nearly every Danish Jew survived the war! And more, the Danes watched over Jewish houses and businesses, so that when the Jews returned after the war they found everything just where they had left it.

In this way, the Danish people earned the name *Hasidei Ummot ha-Olam*, Righteous Gentiles; and won an honored place in the history of the Jews.

A rare photo of Danish Jews being rowed to safety by their Christian neighbors and friends.

21 THE STATE OF ISRAEL

The number of Jews in Palestine kept growing larger. The Jewish National Fund bought more and more land. And the Arabs began to worry that there would come a time when there would be more Jews in Palestine than Arabs. In 1917, in the Balfour Declaration, the British had promised to help the Jews win a homeland in Israel. At the same time, they had made similar promises to the Arabs. So it came to pass that both Jews and Arabs believed that Palestine would some day be theirs, and that Britain would help to make it so.

When the Turks were defeated in World War I, the new League of Nations gave Britain a mandate to rule over Palestine. But the presence of the British government only made things worse. Some Jews began to feel that Britain really wanted to keep Palestine a part of the British empire forever; and some Arabs felt that Britain would stand by no matter what happened between Arabs and Jews. Across Palestine, rioting broke out in which Arabs attacked Jewish settlements. In three hot days in the month of August 1929, more than 530 Jews were either killed or wounded in attacks on Haifa, Tel Aviv, Jerusalem, Hebron, and many small farm settlements. In the 1930s the situation worsened; Arab rioting came more often. And, for the most part, the British did stand by, doing little to halt the rioting.

There were still a few who believed that Arab and Jew could work and build together. The great Jewish thinker, Martin Buber, who had fled Germany in 1938 to settle in Palestine, gave much of his time and energy to teaching that Jews and Arabs could share one state, both being a part of its government. But the Arabs did not trust him; and most Jews did not believe him.

Martin Buber

The Yishuv   For some time, leaders like Weizmann, Ben-Gurion, and Ben-Zvi had been setting up a kind of Jewish government in Palestine to unite all the Zionist political parties. Its "army" was the *Haganah* — a se-

A meeting of Jews and Arabs in 1933: Moshe Shertock, Chaim Weizmann, and David Ben Gurion tried, but could find no formula for real, lasting peace.

cret defense force that had grown out of the *Shomerim* (see chapter nineteen). And the Jews of the *Yishuv* ("Settlement"—the name for the Jewish population of Palestine before the State of Israel was declared) supported both the Haganah and the Jewish Agency, looking to them for leadership.

The Yishuv government was trying its best to bring about a Jewish state through peaceful means. And most Palestinian Jews tried to follow the advice of the leaders of the government, even though they had no official powers. Living in their small farm settlements, they tried to befriend their Arab neighbors—though not always with success. In the cities, Jews lived side by side with Arabs, sharing daily life in business and trade. But Arab leaders, like the Mufti of Jerusalem, taught hatred of the Jews and warned that the Jews would drive the Arabs out of the land completely. And, though these teachings were false, many Arabs believed them. After all, the Mufti was their religious leader. It was a time of confusion and distrust. Arabs, Jews, and British came to hate one another.

Against the best advice of the leaders of the Yishuv, some Jews turned to violence. They called themselves freedom fighters; and they attempted to drive the British out of Pales-

The freedom fighters posted this warning poster (below) to let the British Mandate government know not to publicly whip freedom fighters as the court had ruled.

tine through destroying British offices and property. While it was true that they were terrorists, they acted very differently from terrorists today. They were Jews and they believed in the value of life, so they tried to cause as little bloodshed as possible. In fact, they often warned the British by telephone where and when an attack would take place, so that the British would have time to evacuate. Their object was to drive the British out of Palestine, not to destroy British soldiers. One of the leaders of these terrorists was Menahem Begin who many years later would become prime minister of the State of Israel.

Henrietta Szold and Youth Aliyah

Henrietta Szold was an American who had already done much to help the Yishuv. She was born in Baltimore, Maryland; and studied at the Jewish Theological Seminary, where Conservative rabbis were being trained. For many years she edited *The American Jewish Year Book*, and worked to settle Jewish immigrants coming to the United States. When she heard that the Jews in Palestine were suffering from diseases like malaria, she founded a women's organization called *Hadassah* (named after Queen Esther, who saved her people in Bible times). And Henrietta herself went to Palestine to set up health clinics and hospitals around the country. In 1933, she was given an even greater rescue mission. She became the director of *Youth Aliyah*, an organization that brought 30,000 Jewish young people out of Nazi Europe during the years of persecution, and helped them settle and build new lives in Palestine. For all these great labors, Henrietta Szold became a legend and an inspiration to Jews around the world.

Henrietta Szold

Youth Aliyah training projects.

Aliyah Bet   From 1936 to 1948, the British Mandate Government limited the number of Jews who could enter Palestine. The Arabs had complained that too many Jews were coming. But these were the years of the death camps, and boatloads of Jews who had escaped from Nazi Europe headed toward Palestine hoping to find a new home. The British turned them away, or sent them to the island of Cyprus. On Cyprus, the homeless and bitterly disappointed Jews were placed in guarded camps, behind barbed wires.

To save Jewish lives and to bring more Jews into Palestine, the Haganah smuggled as many Jews as they could into the Holy Land. They brought in the refugees at night, in small boats, sneaking them past the British patrols. This smuggling operation was called *Aliyah Bet*, the "Other" Aliyah, by the Jews. The British called it "illegal immigration." By 1948, one out of every seven Jews in the Yishuv had entered Palestine through Aliyah Bet.

The United Nations Partition Plan   At the end of World War II, the United Nations was set up to replace the old League of Nations. Today the United Nations has become a wasteland of politics with little concern for justice. But in its first years, it made an impressive beginning. It issued a Declaration of Human Rights, and tried to set right some of the suffering that had taken place as a result of the war. None had suffered more than the Jewish people, and in those early and hopeful days the United Nations turned its attention to the question of a Jewish state. A compromise was made called the "Partition Plan." Two states would be carved out of Palestine—one for the Arabs and one for the Jews.

According to the plan, Jerusalem would become an international city to be governed by the United Nations. In this way, Jerusalem would be open to all peoples. The entire world listened by radio as the vote on the Partition Plan was taken in the General Assembly of the United Nations. And

Jewish war veterans take time out to see a then current American movie.

when the vote was complete, the United Nations had approved the plan. The British accepted the vote and made plans to withdraw from Palestine. The Jews accepted the vote, rejoicing that a Jewish state would now be founded legally. But in those days of 1947, the Arabs did not accept the Partition Plan; they began to prepare for war.

Israel's War of Liberation   Even as David Ben-Gurion read aloud the Declaration of Independence of the new State of Israel on May 14, 1948, seven Arab armies were at Israel's borders ready to attack. The Jews of Palestine had no large weapons at all. The Haganah had hidden some guns from the British, but they had no tanks, no large cannon, and no warplanes. The Israeli "air force" was nine private planes. The Arab nations had many more soldiers, modern tanks and guns, and warplanes.

The Egyptians began the war by bombarding Jerusalem from the air. The small Israeli army led by Yaakov Dori and David Ben-Gurion fought battle after desperate battle. Israeli settlements and farm communities held off the advancing Arab armies with homemade mortars and handguns, a few rifles, and some small cannon. Half of Jerusalem, the Old City, was lost to the troops of Jordan. But the war was won.

In March 1949, the Arab armies returned home. But the Arab nations never signed a peace treaty; and they never admitted that Israel had the right to exist.

Building a Nation   There was little time for celebration. From the moment the State was declared, immigrants had come pouring into Israel. Over 340,000 survivors of the death camps came from Europe and Cyprus. More than 200,000 Jews came from Arab lands where most had been oppressed, living poorly for centuries. Many had lived in primitive ghettos called *mellahs*; and some had even lived in caves. So many came so quickly that there was not enough housing. They were sent to live in tent cities called *mabarot*.

A new government was elected. Ben-Gurion became Israel's first prime minister. Weizmann became the first president. A *Knesset* (Assembly) was elected, and the many Zionist parties now became Israel's leadership. Courts of law were set up; and three school systems—public schools, schools for Arabs, and schools for the Orthodox—began teaching. By 1958, the tent cities had disappeared and new immigrants were sent from ships to houses or apartments. The number of kibbutzim and farms grew.

Much teaching was done. Many came who knew no Hebrew; they were taught. Many had never farmed or worked as laborers; they were taught. Many had never seen modern inventions like radio or telephone; they were taught. Some even had to be taught to eat with knives and forks.

Jews of a new kind appeared. They were born in the Holy Land. Their native language was Hebrew. They were called *Sabras*. It was said they were like the Sabra cactus that grows wild in Israel's desert—tough outside, but sweet inside. They grew up learning to fight; and they had to fight many times as the Arab countries continued to attack Israel time and again.

The fruit of a sabra cactus is said to be tough on the outside and sweet on the inside. Native-born Israelis have thus earned the nickname, Sabras. This, then, is a photo of a sabra with a sabra.

A GENERATION OF LEADERS
The men and women who led Israel in its first years were an outstanding group.

David Ben-Gurion (1886– 1973) was born in Russia and came to Palestine when he was twenty. He was a member of the Shomerim, fought with the British army's special Jewish Legion in World War I, and became a leader of Labor Zionism. He was Israel's first prime minister, a member of a kibbutz, a student of Torah, and a writer. In many ways, he was the architect of the new Jewish state.

Isaac Ben-Zvi (1884– 1963) was a founder of the Shomerim, fought with the Jewish Legion, and helped lead the Labor Zionists. In 1948 he founded a school to study the Jewish communities in Arab lands (now called the Ben-Zvi Institute); and in 1952 he became the second president of Israel.

Rachel Yanait Ben-Zvi (1886– 1984), wife of Isaac was an important leader in her own right. She was a member of the Shomerim, a pioneer of the Women's Labor Movement, and a leader in the Haganah. She studied farming; and founded a school of agriculture for women near Jerusalem.

Abba Eban (1915-   ) was born in South Africa and studied in England. In 1948 he became Israel's first representative in the United Nations, later Israel's ambassador to the United States. Afterward, he was minister of education and culture and then foreign minister of Israel. He wrote many books, the most famous being *My People, A History of the Jews.*

Golda Meir (1898– 1979) was born in Russia, grew up in Milwaukee, Wisconsin, became a Labor leader in Palestine, and was sent in 1948 to be Israel's first ambassador to Russia. For many years after that she was a member of the Knesset; and she became prime minister in 1969. She served as prime minister through the Yom Kippur War of 1973, in difficult times, but her warmth and kindness held the nation together.

Yigael Yadin (1917–   ) was born in Palestine, the son of a famous archaeologist. As a member of the Haganah he helped plan Israel's defense in the War of Independence, and became commander of Israel's Defense Forces in 1949. Later he taught archaeology at the Hebrew University, led the famous digs at Hazor and Masada, and served as deputy prime minister.

22 ISRAEL TODAY

Years of War The Arab countries surrounding Israel forced the Israelis to fight one war after another. In 1956, Egypt blocked the straits of Teran, stopping ships from coming to Israel's southern port, Eilat. The Israelis, along with the British and the French, fought a war to open the Suez Canal. In 1967, Arab armies threatened Israel from the north and south; and another war was fought. This became known as the Six Day War, because Israel's armed forces moved so quickly they defeated the Arabs in six days.

In the Six Day War, the capital city of Jerusalem was reunited. The Old City had fallen into the hands of Jordan in 1948, and the Jordanians had forbidden Jews to enter it. Now it was reconquered by Israel and the two halves of Jerusalem joined together. Jews, Christians, and Arabs alike were allowed to visit all the holy places of Jerusalem; and Jews could once more visit the holiest of all Jewish places, the Western Wall, the last remains of the ancient Temple.

It was while the Jews of Israel were at prayer on Yom Kippur day in 1973 that the next war began. The armies of Egypt and Syria launched a surprise attack meant to drive the Jews of Israel into the sea. And they almost succeeded. Israeli

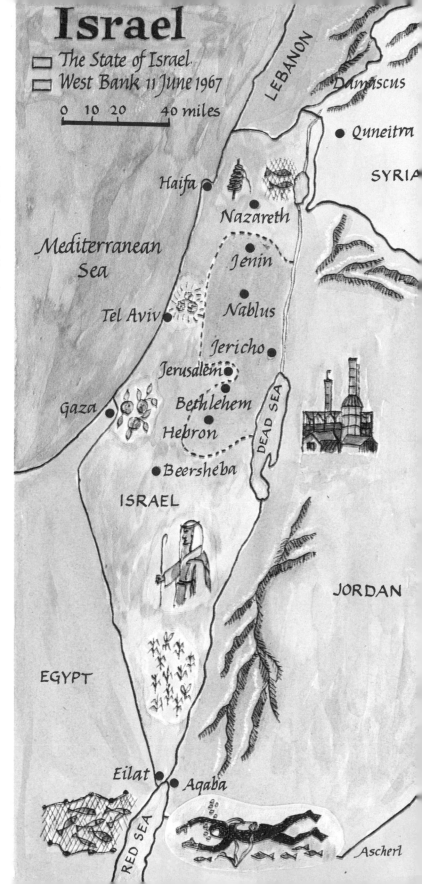

Israel

□ The State of Israel
□ West Bank 11 June 1967

0 10 20   40 miles

reserves had not been called up, and the Israeli armed forces were not prepared for a war. And the Arabs fought more fiercely than they ever had before. The Jews of the world were shocked when only one nation—the United States—came to the aid of Israel in this dangerous moment. After many military setbacks, the Israelis managed to win. But the cost was high. There was hardly a family in Israel that had not lost one of its children or one of its close friends.

The Palestinians During these years of conflict, another problem was developing. When Israel was created, many Arabs fled their homes in Palestine, hoping to return after the Arab armies had defeated the Jews. The Jews, however, were not defeated; and the Arab nations kept these "Palestinian" Arabs in refugee camps along Israel's borders. A whole generation of young Arabs was raised in these camps, taught that their true home was in the land held by the Jews, and taught to hate the Jews of Israel. Instead of being settled to become citizens of other Arab lands, they were trained by the Arab governments to become fierce soldiers. At night, and by surprise during the day, Palestinian terrorists slipped across the borders to attack Israeli villages and towns. They killed men, women, and children alike. They wanted not just to have their homes again, but to destroy the Israeli people entirely.

In 1972, the Palestinian terrorists attacked the Israeli athletic team at the Munich Olympics in Germany. They killed every Israeli who fell into their hands. For a brief moment the world was stunned. But the games went on as scheduled; and the world forgot. In 1976, terrorists hijacked a French airliner carrying many Israeli passengers. They flew it to Entebbe airport in Uganda. It seemed they would kill all the Israelis and Jews there, too. But this time Israel was ready. In a surprise attack, thousands of miles from home, the Israelis rescued the hostages and brought nearly all of them away safely. Palestinian terrorists continue to attack Israel today; and Israel is still forced to fight back.

Morning prayer for a soldier in the field: Sinai Campaign, 1956.

The Hope for Peace   In 1977, an important step was taken toward bringing peace to the Middle East. President Anwar Sadat of Egypt came to Jerusalem to speak to the Israeli Knesset. Egypt had been Israel's worst enemy through the many years of war; and it was a moment that few believed would ever come.

Afterward, Sadat and Begin, Israel's prime minister, continued to meet. A year and a half later, a historic conference took place at Camp David in the United States. Together with President Jimmy Carter of the United States, Sadat and Begin signed a first treaty of peace between their two countries. To many of us watching television at that moment, it was a great day: Christian (Carter), Jew (Begin), and Muslim

(Sadat) had met together and from that meeting came the hope of peace! Many things had still to be settled, and it would be many years before peace could really be achieved—if ever. The rest of the Arab nations called Sadat a traitor; and a short time later, Sadat was murdered by Arab assassins.

A Problem for the Future   The Israeli Jews built a nation in a wilderness. They passed a law stating that Israel is the home of any Jew who wishes to come. Wherever they farmed, the land was green. Their cities were modern. The kibbutzim turned to factory work as well as farm work. Israelis produced their own automobiles, sold their Jaffa oranges to other countries, became famous for their diamond-cutting industry, and designed and built their own warplanes. Their army weapon, the hand-held *uzzi* machine gun, was sold to many other countries. At the same time, many Israelis began to feel they were losing touch with their Jewishness. While some were Orthodox, many had little to do with religion.

The Orthodox Jews had long before formed Zionist political parties that gained power in the new state. Only Orthodox rabbis were allowed to perform marriages and other Jewish ceremonies, even for Jews who were not religious; and only the Orthodox were allowed to judge how Judaism should be practiced in the state. While the concerns of building a new state had been uppermost, this seemed no problem, but now many Israelis began searching for a *Toda'ah Yehudit*, a self-understanding of their Jewish identity.

Israelis began to ask new questions like: What does it mean to be a Jew in Israel? How should Israeli Jews feel toward Jews in the Diaspora? What should Israelis teach their children about Judaism? Two movements from America, Conservative and Reform Judaism, set up centers in Israel. But the rabbis of these movements soon discovered that they would have to work for a new kind of religious freedom within the Jewish state—a freedom for Jews in Israel to choose how they wish to be Jewish.

ISRAEL AND ARCHAEOLOGY

Since the time of the Yishuv, Israel has been digging into its past. The Dead Sea Scrolls were discovered in 1947. They were pieces of the Bible almost two thousand years old; and studying them proved that the words of the Bible had been copied faithfully from that time to this! The scrolls also provided hints about the lives of the Essenes, a group that lived near the Dead Sea at the time of Hillel and Shammai. But this was just the beginning.

Farmers plowing their fields found remains of ancient Israel. Round-topped hills, *tels*, were the ruins of cities mentioned in the Bible and other ancient writings. Israelis became amateur archaeologists. They learned how ancient peoples had defended the land and where the strongest forts had been built and the best roads laid down. They studied how the land had been farmed in ancient times; and learned how water had been collected even in the dry desert, and crops grown where little rain ever fell. And they used what they discovered of the past in rebuilding the land.

Discovering the past, digging where the people of Judah and Israel had lived long before, gave modern Israelis a sense of having returned home at last. They learned to take pride in the past. And they explored the land not only with maps and guidebooks, but with shovels and brushes in one hand and copies of the Bible in the other.

23 THE JEWISH WORLD TODAY

There was a time when it seemed that Jewish communities could be found no matter where in the world one traveled. Jewish communities had flourished in strange places like K'ai-feng in China, Cochin in India, Yokohama in Japan, Kingston in Jamaica, and San'a in Yemen. Some, like K'ai-feng and Dura-Europus (in what is now Syria) and Alexandria (in Egypt) had disappeared long before modern times. The Holocaust swept away the great communities of Eastern Europe and greatly reduced the Jewish communities of Western Europe, too. Arab persecution forced the Jews of North Africa to leave in large numbers, especially after the birth of the State of Israel. Today, the largest Jewish communities are in the United States, in Israel, and in Russia. There are major communities in England, France, and Argentina, and smaller communities still remain in places like Australia, India, Peru, Mexico, Central America, even Germany. In many of these, Jews live in freedom among their neighbors, but the age-old struggle against hatred and oppression is still far from over.

The Jews of Yemen   A considerable number of Jews lived in Yemen from the third century C.E. on. In those days, this South Arabian country was called Himyar, and tradition has it that several kings of Himyar and many of its citizens adopted Judaism. The last Jewish king was put to death by raiding Abyssinians in the late sixth century; and by the seventh century, the country fell into the hands of the Muslims. Anti-Jewish laws were passed, and the community was heavily taxed. From time to time the Jews were persecuted—once an entire community of Jews was sent out to the desert to starve. The heavy taxes and the persecutions brought the Jews to the point, in the twelfth century, where many began to put their faith in a false Messiah. The chief rabbi of Yemen sent an urgent letter to Maimonides, asking the great rabbi what should be done. Maimonides replied that the Jews should reject the false

A Yemenite Jew practices the art of making jewelry. Yemenite jewelry is known for its delicacy and beauty. Below, a Yemenite Jew creates another kind of delicate design.

The Yemenite Jews, rescued from a backwater of the world, have become a colorful and important part of the people of Israel today. Here, in native costumes, is a Yemenite picnic.

Messiah and put their trust in God. One day, the sage said, God would return the Jews of Yemen to the Holy Land. Copies of the letter were sent to every Jewish community in Yemen, and the Jews turned away from following the false Messiah and put their hope in the future.

Far away from the centers of Judaism, the Yemenite Jews lived their lives almost as if the days of the Bible had never passed. Most of them were crafters — gold and silversmiths, jewellers, basket weavers, potters, carpenters, blacksmiths, gunsmiths, and saddlers. The women embroidered beautiful clothing. Children were taught to read Hebrew — and since books were scarce and each school might have only one or two, it was said that a Yemenite child could read Hebrew upside down, rightside up, or sideways.

In 1869, when the Suez Canal was opened, Yemen was once again connected to the modern world. When the Jews of Yemen heard in the 1880s that Zionists were settling in Palestine, they believed that this was the beginning of the great promised return to the Holy Land. Many Yemenite Jews set off for Israel to settle there. Conditions in Yemen grew more severe when the country became independent in 1911, and that, too, was a reason to leave. By 1948, some 18,000 Yemenite Jews had come to join the Yishuv.

But it was the birth of the new State of Israel that finally freed the Jews of Yemen. From 1949 to 1950, the Israelis brought almost the whole of the remaining Jewish community to the Holy Land by airplane. The Yemenites had long believed that God would bring them home "on the wings of eagles," and now felt that the promises of the ancient Covenant and the faith of Maimonides had been rewarded. Today the Jews of Yemen are a unique part of Israeli culture, for they brought with them their wonderful sense of dance and song, their rare abilities as craftspeople, and their talents in the making of fine clothing.

Beta Israel   Since the time of the first Temple, a group of Jews called the *Falashas* (they call themselves "Beta Israel," the House of Israel) lived among African tribes in what is now Ethiopia. For hundreds of years at a time, they were cut off from any contact with the Jewish people, yet they followed loyally the laws of Torah, and believed they were a part of the Chosen People of Israel. Every once in a while, they were "rediscovered" by one Jewish traveler or another; then forgotten again as history swept past them.

In the nineteenth century, one of their leaders nearly became a modern Moses. He told his people to sell their homes and pack their belongings and to follow him to the Holy Land. The long march began in joy, but ended in tragedy as thousands of Falashas died long before reaching the African coast. In the end, saddened by defeat, the Ethiopian Jews returned to their tribal villages and picked up their lives as best they could.

Today they live in the worst kind of poverty, tortured by disease and starvation. Local government leaders are cruelly anti-Semitic, refusing either to allow the Beta Israel to leave Ethiopia or to practice their religion freely. Nevertheless, a few thousand have escaped. Some have made their way to Israel. Others are trapped in refugee camps in Africa. In 1982, the State of Israel promised to rescue the Falashas; and Jews the world over began to support these efforts.

Young women of the Beta Israel study at a nursing school. Back in Ethiopia, their trapped relatives and friends still follow primitive tribal customs.

Russian Jewry   Still another great rescue story taking place today concerns the Jews of Russia. Although there was a large Russian Jewish community even before World War II, many thousands of Jews fleeing the Nazis entered Russia during the war, making the Jewish community there the second largest in the world. Unfortunately, the Jews found that they had escaped one trap only to fall into another. The Communists who rule Russia proved almost as cruel as the Nazis.

Russian Jews carry identity cards that mark them as

Left—two arrivals: On the top, Morrocan Jews entering Israel. On the bottom, Russian Jews arriving at Israel's Ben Gurion airport to breathe the air of freedom.

On the right—two folk festivals: Morrocan and Kurdistani Jews share their cultures.

Jewish, but Judaism—the practice of the Jewish religion—has been outlawed. The government forbids the printing of Jewish books, the training of new rabbis, the publishing of Jewish newspapers, and even the making of matzah for Passover. Jews are forced to be Jews, but not allowed to be Jewish. Once there were thousands of synagogues in Russia; today there are about sixty. Once there were thousands of rabbis in Russia; today there are just a handful. Jewish leaders

are often sent to Soviet prison camps to endure long years of hardship and starvation in Siberian wastelands just for teaching Hebrew.

Officially, the Communist government allows some Jews to leave. But choosing to go is a dangerous matter. A few are given exit visas, while others are refused over and over again. These Jews call themselves "Refuseniks"; their lives are made bitter by the government. Usually they lose their jobs, their telephones may be taken away, mail does not always reach them. They may be sent to prison for the "crime" of being out of a job. But they are brave. They study Hebrew and Jewish history; they copy out books about Judaism by hand and pass them around; they meet together to talk about being Jewish; and they secretly teach their children in nurseries and Hebrew schools. They paste pictures of Israel and Jewish celebrations on their walls, and they dream of leaving Russia. Some have carried this dream as their hope through as many as ten years of trouble.

Nearly 1,700,000 Jews live in Russia and the Soviet Republics today. No one knows how many wish to leave, but the number seems to be growing day by day. For those who manage to get out, there is help waiting to take them to Israel or to the United States where they can find ways of living new lives of freedom.

Other Jewish Problems   In Arab lands, especially in Syria, Iraq and Iran, Jews suffer from vicious anti-Semitism. Often they are not allowed to leave, yet hatred is wrapped around them, choking them, trying to destroy them. The situation is very different in South Africa, where Jews are allowed to leave for Israel. Many would like to go on aliyah but do not wish to leave behind everything they own and have worked for.

And in some countries of South America, Jews have equal rights under law, but social pressures and sometimes governments fall into the hands of Communists, particularly; the practice of Judaism and the lives of the Jews can become difficult and dangerous.

In the Lands of Freedom   Of course, many Jews today live in lands of freedom, where they are accepted as equals. In these lands—the United States, some countries of South America, England, Australia, Canada—the Jews are not separated physically from their neighbors or even made to feel separate. Here, the struggle is not to overcome hatred, but to protect the Jewish communities from assimilation. Often Jewish education is weak and young people drift away from Judaism, hardly knowing what kind of treasure they are giving up. For the most part, however, Judaism is alive and well in these lands; and where freedom and equality are truly practiced, Jews often make strong contributions to the well-being of their nations and of the Jewish people around the world.

Today, more than at any other time in Jewish history, we know how cruel anti-Semitism can be. We know what has happened to our people before; we have read about and witnessed the Holocaust and its terrors. And we have pledged—all Jews pledged—to help one another so that such things may never happen again anywhere. We remind ourselves of this pledge with a motto: *Kol Yisrael Arevin Zeh Bazeh,* "Every Jew is responsible for every other."

Where Jews Live Today

The world's population of Jews is about 13,000,000. Most live in the United States, Israel, and the Soviet Union (Russia). These are the major Jewish communities of the world today and how many Jews are in each:

5,690,000	United States	108,000	South Africa
3,282,700	Israel	70,000	Australia
1,700,000	Soviet Union	65,000	Hungary
535,000	France	40,000	Uruguay
390,000	Great Britain	35,000	Mexico
308,000	Canada	33,500	West Germany
242,000	Argentina	33,000	Belgium
110,000	Brazil	33,000	Rumania

[These 1980 figures are from the AMERICAN JEWISH YEAR BOOK, 1982.]

24 JEWS IN THE UNITED STATES TODAY

The Jewish community of the United States is the largest Jewish community in history. Though some United States Jews are poor, most are a part of the middle class—engineers, architects, teachers, lawyers, dentists, physicians, accountants, business people, scientists, musicians, writers, and artists. Few speak Yiddish, the language of their Eastern European past; but many study Hebrew. There are Jewish newspapers and magazines; Jewish synagogues and organizations. Bible, Talmud, Midrash, and many other Jewish classics can be read in English; and Jews are free to teach and study them in Jewish schools.

There has been anti-Semitism in the United States. Jews were sometimes kept out of "exclusive" clubs or hotels or neighborhoods. But the government has never been anti-Semitic, and open anti-Semitism has been rare in recent years.

Once it was hoped that citizens of the United States would forget their past in places like Europe, Africa, and Asia and join a "melting pot" in which all would become one "American" people, thinking and acting alike. But democracy has come to mean more than that. The past is now seen as a great natural resource that all can share. Each group is free to search for its roots and to develop its culture, and to share that culture with other groups. Americans have learned to use their freedom to enrich one another; and American Jews are no exception.

The Coming of Freedom—The First Event Three great world events shaped the Jewish community in America. The first was the declaration of American independence, and its guarantee of liberty and justice for all.

Using this freedom to create and build, the Jews of the United States have been successful in almost every walk of life. There have been great Jewish scientists, teachers, physicians, artists, judges, lawyers, business people, publishers,

Albert Einstein,
physicist

Arthur Golderg,
lawyer and diplomat

Henry J. Kissinger,
diplomat and scholar

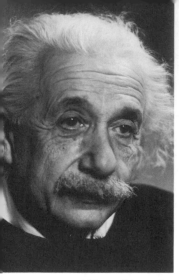

Barbra Streisand, en-
tertainer and singer

Danny Kaye, actor

actors, musicians, photographers, writers, and sports figures. Names like Albert Einstein, Saul Bellow, Bernard Baruch, Al Jolson, Louis B. Mayer, Molly Picon, the Marx Brothers, Danny Kaye, George Gershwin, Barbra Streisand, Harry Austryn Wolfson, Maurce Samuel, Jennie Grossinger, Ben Shahn, Isaac Bashevis Singer, Arthur Goldberg, Helena Rubinstein, Harry Houdini, Barney Ross, Sandy Koufax, and Henry Kissinger are just a few of the thousands who have been outstanding in their fields. Through their creative use of freedom, they have been able to make contributions to the modern world as a whole.

The Holocaust—The Second Event

Although the Holocaust occurred decades ago, only recently have Jews understood its meaning. We lost six million of our people, the yeshivot and centers of study in Europe, and a way of life—its language and its traditions. Now we study what was lost, rediscovering it, learning from it. Today we must live with the terrible knowledge that wherever Jews suffer it is especially the duty of American Jews—the largest, richest, and most secure community—to come to their aid.

The Birth of Israel—The Third Event

In the lifetimes of many of us, a miracle has occurred. The State of Israel has been reborn. The American Jewish community helps to support and maintain the new state. But Israel's Jews have a voice of their own and a mind of their own. Like members of the same family, the Jews of America and the Jews of Israel share love and friendship and sometimes, disagreement. In the end, our two communities are building the future of Judaism. This building is the Covenant in action.

Changes in American Judaism When the immigrants—especially those from Eastern Europe—first arrived, they struggled to be a part of American society. They needed to earn a living, give education to their children, rise above their lower class beginnings. Recently, American Jews have turned more attention to the task of creating a new Jewish life-style.

Leading Jewish thinkers debate how religion, God, and peoplehood—the Covenant—affect our everyday lives. In the past, they concentrated on human actions and Jewish writings. Now we find that discovering the real meaning of the Covenant with God has a new importance for us.

Synagogues continue to be central to Judaism in America, but a new movement called the *Havurah* (Hebrew for a community of friends) is growing. Small groups meet together for worship and study and for social pleasure, trying to make Judaism central in their lives. In a time when family life is threatened through wide-spread divorce and separation of generations by distances, these *Havurot* have a feeling of old-time family gatherings.

Women are also seeking new roles. There are Reform and Reconstructionist women serving as rabbis; and others taking active parts as synagogue officers, presidents, and cantors. Women are often called to the Torah for aliyot and counted as part of the minyan (the ten people needed for worship) in Reform, Reconstructionist, and many Conservative synagogues.

And American Jews have demanded new and more modern prayer books and new and more modern editions of the Haggadah for Passover. Many of these have been issued by the official movements and include beautiful and lyrical

Scenes in Jewish education. Left: In the library of a day school. Center: A Hebrew classroom. Right: Studying ethics and values.

translations of traditional prayers, modern poetry and prayers, and lovely illustrations. Even a new and modern translation of the Bible has recently been completed.

The Future? Some say the future looks very bright for American Jews; some say it does not. There is assimilation, and some Jews are lost to Judaism through intermarriage—but these are not new things in the Jewish journey. As Jews move out of the major cities and spread more thinly through the United States, they lose some of their power in politics—yet they still have a voice through their national movements and organizations. It is often said that few Jews go to synagogue regularly, yet the synagogues continue to be supported, and almost all Jews feel it is important that their children get a Jewish education.

As a matter of fact, it is in the area of Jewish education that things look brightest for the future. Many Jewish children attend day schools, where Judaism is taught along with science, math, English, and other subjects. More and more adults come to hear Jewish speakers or to take courses in Judaism at their synagogues. And the network of Jewish charitable organizations that began when the Jews first made their promise to Peter Stuyvesant that they would never be a burden on the Christian community, has grown into the strongest force for tzedakah that has ever existed.

The future, of course, is in your hands. If you have read and studied carefully, you have learned much about what our people believes and how it lives. You have discovered the things that keep us apart, and the things that make us one. And you can help decide the future. You are the Jewish future.